AF480857

The Power of Your Altar

of Your Altar

NADINE MCARTHUR

TABLE OF CONTENTS

INTRODUCTION

I authored this book from a place of victory. A place of: "God did it and it's already done!" Though, while at the beginning of drafting this book, I had not yet seen the manifestation, the faith walker in me believed the word of the Lord, that it was already done. I knew I had shifted from my season of testing to my season of promise.

Yes, there were signs that I was still experiencing some residue from the old season, but I trusted God. I knew He wanted me to pen my transparent testimony to encourage someone who may be experiencing a similar test or entering their season of promise, who could use a "cheat sheet" to get through the debris.

My cheat sheet was discovering the POWER of my altar. Now, don't get me wrong, I've always been a person of prayer but truly didn't understand the power I had on my altar.

Many believers pray for hours and yet still we walk around feeling defeated, because we do not understand the secrets of the altar. It is that expression that says: "I was today years old when I discovered that… all along I was doing it wrong!"

Well today, I will share my story and some things I have learned, along with the tools that brought results.

Psalm 45:1 (KJV), says, "My heart is inditing a good matter: I speak of the things which I have made touching the king: My tongue is the pen of a ready writer." Since you are holding this book in your hands, please know that you are holding what is equivalent to a treasure box full of wonderful jewels and nuggets that God has allowed me to pen just for you! That's how special you are to Him.

I pray you take the time to open the box, or the book if you will, and allow your spirit to absorb what you need. Now I know the contents may not be for everyone, but I pray that the right person gets their hands on this book. My prayer is that it will shift someone's life in the direction it needs to go.

With that said, grab that glass of lemonade or hot cocoa and journey with me as we uncover, "The Power of Your Altar."

CHAPTER ONE:
THE BACKDROP

Being vulnerable costs! Vulnerability comes from the transparency of your testimony. Let me spell that again: "TEST-TEA-MONEY." There are three parts to this word.

There's the first part of the word: "TEST". This is the part where you're experiencing something painful, otherwise known as the tough situation. You are being tested, and testing hurt! It leaves you afraid, vulnerable and embarrassed. And then as if that's not enough we have the "TEA" where it leaves you feeling exposed, so much you become the subject of everyone's conversation. Folks will have so much to say about what they perceive you are going through. Or they will be quick to suggest what to do because if they were you, they would do this, that or the other. Easier said than done when you are not the one going through the test.

One can only speculate, not knowing the truth because they are not walking in your shoes. They will have everything to say about you and the situation. Everything that is, except a prayer or word of encouragement. But the good news is, if you can endure the TEST and the TEA and fight to get the MONEY, I promise you, you will embrace the blessing that follows.

"MONEY" represents the blessed place. It represents the reward for having endured the trials (test) and the gossip (tea). It is the manifestation of the promise. All three together make up the word "testimony".

While building your testimony is not a comfortable or easy task, I encourage you that once you have overcome the process do what Jesus told Peter: "strengthen your brethren" (read Luke 22:31-32). Your testimony ought to be the very thing that encourages someone else to the finish line.

It will cost you something to be transparent and to open up publicly about your pain. But it will be more costly to the ones who are assigned to your voice if you keep silent. Mordecai said it best to Esther: "For if you remain silent at this time, relief and deliverance for the Jews will arise from another place...." Can God trust YOU to share? Can He trust you to open up your mouth to provoke someone else's deliverance, even if it cost you everything, including your life? Sit and ponder about that for a second.

We can be the most private, non-witnessing, self-centered believers at times. When we read scripture, we read about some very personal, private, intimate, humiliating and controversial parts of the characters' stories. How embarrassed would they be if they were to walk into the churches today and hear pastors dissecting their stories and preaching all their business in front of multitudes of people in person and online? How exposing! But we thank God that we have a cloud of witnesses that has gone before us whose testimonies are still available to us to help us through our tough situations. Some didn't even live to experience the manifestation. But we have word and proof to help us navigate our Christian journey.

Now, let me ask the question again and before you respond I want you to pause and consider what it would cost you to give God your "yes." The question again is: "Can God trust you to share your testimony?"

The Bible says in Revelations 12:11, "And they overcame him by the blood of the Lamb, and by the word of their testimony; and they loved not their lives unto the death."

I promised the Lord a long time ago that if He allowed me to go through the hard thing, as much as I don't like it, I will submit to the testand allow Him to process me.When He does, and when I come out of the situation, I promise to turn around and help someone else through whatever it is they are facing. I don't know if that's why sometimes I feel like I experience so much. Could it be, He's enjoying getting the glory out of my life a bit much? I chuckle when I say that. But the truth is, He knows my heart that I want nothing more than to put a smile on His face while seeing His people set free and delivered.

CHAPTER 2:
THE DISCOVERY

As mentioned previously, this book was birthed at the end of a very pivotal season in my life. It was at a time when I experienced things which I had only heard of. At the time, I had been married for approximately 3 years and had yet to enjoy the honeymoon stages of my marriage.

Prior to marrying my spouse, I knew him for approximately 10 years. At the time we started dating, we were in a very crucial time in the world: we were experiencing a pandemic known as COVID-19. During that time millions of lives were lost. My spouse and I both suffered the loss of our grandmothers who also passed away from non-Covid circumstances approximately 2 months apart.

One day, a conversation about ministry led us to a conversation about our grandmothers. We realized then how much of a legacy each had contributed to our lives. That particular conversation kept us on the phone for well over 2 hours and brought us closer together. We would frequently talk for hours for the next few weeks until one day he asked me out on an unofficial date. He asked me to go with him to a clothing store to make a return which ended up being a nice evening hanging out afterwards.

He was very respectful, kind and funny. I experienced another side of him that I hadn't seen in the years I had known him. He was always a "nice guy," but I got to see his heart a bit more. I had the privilege of hearing his story about his past. He opened up about his dreams and aspirations and our connection grew as I realize how muchwe had in common. Our dating quickly turned into courtship and next thing we know in just 4 months we were married.

Now almost immediately after saying "I do," my husband went from being "in love" to becoming distant and cold. I can't say that something specific happened. Yes, we had "moments" like any new relationships, but the behaviorbecame very peculiar in that it's as if his heart completely waxed cold towards me. He began repelling me as his wife. At the time, I didn't think of it as any outside interference. Instead, I just thought we had just made a huge mistake. Stick with me there is a reason I am being so detailed with my story.

Months later,I received aprophetic wordthat there were several witches working against our marriage. Now I wasn't one of those folks that concentrated on witches/witchcraft. In my mind, yes they exist, but I didn̓t place too much thought around them.I was told that one of the witches did something to turn my husband's spirit against me because if she could not have him, she was going to make sure I wouldn't enjoy my marriage.

We also had several other prophesies that God had a great outreach ministry for us to do but the enemy is going to try to sift the marriage to derail the plan that God has for our ministry and ultimately, our destiny. Now, I heard these words but didn't take them as seriously as I should have. Can I tell you, as a believer I didn't even pray against what was revealed. That was a very costly mistake!

Here is the first golden nugget: Bathe your relationship in prayer. I would pray for the obvious things: blessings over my spouse, for his needs and desires to be met and so on, but I did not understand the depth of prayer I needed to pray against spiritual warfare. I didn't fully understand spiritual warfare as it pertains to marriage. I had no clue how far the enemy would go to separate one's relationship, not because he is intimidated by you as a mere couple but because he is afraid of you as a "kingdom couple." There is a significant difference! He understands that kingdom couples have great assignments and so he will stop at nothing to destroy the covenant made between the couple and the Lord. He understands that such a marriage has purpose, and that's what he's after, the purpose!

I admonish you, pray about EVERYTHING. Don't wait until you've received an adverse word about your relationship, but especially then, increase the fire on your altar! Let prayer be the guide to lead you into the right relationship and to sustain you while you're in it. Allow your prayers to form a barrier around you, your spouse and your home. Do not take my words lightly. I endured it, survived it and now here to prevent you from experiencing what I went through, if you'll heed. Again, I say pray, pray… and then when you're done praying, pray some more!

CHAPTER 3:
THE COST OF IGNORANCE

As a person from the Caribbean who has heard of witches and witchcraft, I was so ignorant to the demonic realm. I thought that if I didn't focus on that stuff, it couldn't affect me. Boy was I ignorant and inaccurate! Well, even though it could not affect me directly, it certainly affected me indirectly! In the end it caused much damage to my relationship.

The thing that brought my spouse and I together was ministry, but it had now become the thing that separated us. I could not understand. How could my "kingdom husband" despise the ministry or minister in me to which he was drawn? Was it all a front? Why God, did you allow this after I waited this long to be married? While single, I prayed for my spouse. I wanted who God had for me. Now after having waited, here I was now facing all this warfare.

Right before we started seeing each other, in the middle of a pandemic, I received five prophecies back-to-back, over a period of 5 months that my husband was already around me, and I was to prepare as it would be a very short courtship. Exactly what was prophesied, was what happened. There were so many confirmations that God sanctioned my marriage. One prophetic word even went as far as saying that we didn't choose each other. We had other people and plans in mind, but God ordained the marriage and put us together because He had a greater purpose for our union.

Now, keep in mind the title of this book "The Power of Your Altar" as everything I'm sharing will hopefully come full circle and make sense by the time you're done reading.

Now as I remember, during the first year of marriage, we immediately began to have issues. There was a young lady who was a friend of my husband who was always around him. This young lady was a "minister" and eventually was ordained a pastor. Saints be careful of those who pretend to be sheep but are nothing but wolves in sheep's clothing. Also keep in mind this book is not intended to destroy anyone's character but to shed light and truth regarding the wickedness and subtleness of the enemy.

This young lady was friends with my husband long before we even considered dating. She would be his "sounding board" whenever we were dealing with situations in our marriage. Random days she would text him "I'm here for you and I'm praying for you." "You were in my spirit today. I'm praying for you". Of course he was in her spirit. She was obsessed with my husband, but he couldn't see it. He genuinely saw her as his friend with whom he could confide.

This young lady was well known for intercession at her local church. I wanted to add this here to say witches are not always unbelievers outside of church. They are folks leading the prayer groups, preaching on platforms. They are folks who show up and present themselves as "spiritual." They speak in tongues; they pray up a storm and can preach circles around you! Don't be fooled by the gifts. Gifts come without repentance. Even though you are born with certain gifts, they can become contaminated. God will not revoke your gifts because you are walking in disobedience.

I encourage you to try the spirit by the spirit. Don't be fooled by theatrics and the art of ministry. Folks have learned to "master their craft," and crafty they are! Use discernment with the folks around you. Be careful who you trust, everyone is not close because they are celebrating you. Some stay close as monitoring spirit to study your next move. Be careful who you share your heart with and from whom you eat food. Guard your heart, your home and your platform (the space where God uses you to minister). Be wise and be prayerful.

A year into our marriage, two prophets spoke the same word separately to me that there were two witches around me that did not want my marriage to work. I was told that one of the witches decided that if she couldn't have my husband, I would never enjoy my marriage. Now, hearing these prophesies, the young woman did cross my mind. But not taking it seriously I dismissed it. There were times she would show up and I would exchange words with her about her not respecting my marriage. Eventually she pulled away …or so it seems.

Two years later she resurfaced to compliment me via text about the work I was doing in the ministry. Because time had elapsed since we last exchanged heated words, I thought she had moved on, and it was time to make peace.

I picked up the phone to call her to thank her for her "kind" words but also to apologize for the exchange of unpleasant words we had two years prior. In her response she said something along these lines "Oh I didn't reach out to fix things between us. I reached out to compliment your work. You see, how I feel about your husband hasn't changed. In fact, your problem is that you have an issue with the fact that I'm still in love with him. You need to get over it. I've been in love with him before you two ever got together!" Needless to say, that conversation ended but again it didn't end well.

Shortly after, my husband and I started falling apart again. My voice irritated him, my presence irritated him. He was annoyed by what I was doing in ministry even though we were pastoring together at our local church.During that time, I remembered the prophesy from some time ago: "The witch set your husband's spirit against yours. She decided that if she couldn't have him, you will never enjoy your marriage." Now I'm not passing blame on a third party for our marriage going in the wrong direction. There were things we could have done differently as well. But as I said I'm sharing for a reason.

Over the next few months, I watched my marriage go under and eventually we completely separated. My husband was now out of the home. The young lady was not around so of course I would not suspect her of having anything to do with it. And maybe, she didn't have anything to do with him leaving.

I began to blame my husband for his behavior, and rightfully so in some regard. He and I weren't handling things well. In hindsight, there were things we both could have done differently outside of the interference we experienced. I also recognized that there was an unseen hand working behind the scenes that I had overlooked…satan himself.

Many times, we are focused on the behaviors of the person, but we miss the master manipulator behind the scenes with the puppet strings using the people to carry out his treacherous acts. People are not the enemy. They are simply vessels who avail themselves to be used by the real enemy, Satan the deceiver, implementing acts of wickedness.

Satan wants us to overlook his influence in manipulating our day-to-day affairs and our lives on a whole. We become so caught up in what's happening and the person doing wrong that we forget that we have an adversary working against us who is trying to get access to our souls: mind, emotions and our will. His plan is to steal, kill and destroy. In many cases he knows he cannot convince us to backslide, but he will do his best to derail us from God's plan for our lives.

Whenever we see warfare happening around us, we need to go behind the scenes and investigate what is taking place in the realm of the spirit. We need to know what demonic spirit and/or activity is working against us. Where and how was access granted and how can we close those doors? We will go into this more as we get further in this book.

CHAPTER 4:
THE UNFOLDING OF WHAT WAS HAPPENING BEHIND THE SCENES

During the time of separation from my spouse, I felt broken. That was when I really started to pray. Not because I was so spiritual, but as you may know, sometimes the fire sends you running to the altar out of desperation. At least if you are truly a child of the King, when hell breaks loose in your life, it should send you running to Abba for help.

So, I began to weep before the Lord: "Lord why did you allow this?" "How did I miss you in agreeing to this marriage?" "Was this even you?" "What could I have done differently?" I needed answers. I needed God to fix my marriage. I needed him to deal with my husband. "Why Lord, why?!"

As I began to cry out to God, asking Him questions, it seems as if God was responding to me about everything except my marriage. It's almost as if He was talking around my situation, but not addressing it directly. But what I didn't know was that God in His all-wise sovereignty was weaving all the pieces together. I just could not understand it. He was doing more than answering those basic questions. He was piecing my entire LIFE together! Keep reading, I promise it will bless you.

So, as I continued praying out of desperation, one morning around 5am, I had a strange dream. Now as I share the dream it's important that you pay close attention to what seems like insignificant details in the dream. It will all make sense throughout this book.

I dreamt that I was in an apartment building like the one I lived in as a teenager, on the fourth floor. In the dream, the apartment I was in was filthy, but it wasn't covered with garbage. The floors were instead covered with dirty clothes. Everywhere you looked there were dirty clothes. In the corner of the room was my husband lying on a sheet-less, dirty mattress resting directly on the floor. My husband seemed to be in some form of a trance and was unaware of what was happening in the room. I walked over to sit next to him on the mattress and he was completely oblivious of my presence.

Moments later, an unseen hand handed me a chocolate brown clutch (purse). I didn't see the face of the person who gave it to me. I was excited to accept the gift and immediately opened it up to see what was on the inside. When I opened it, I saw what looked like beautiful ribbons. The ribbons were multicolored pink and blue and almost seemed to be made from a material that was like glass, (bear with me this is dream world, anything is possible).

I started pulling the beautiful ribbons out of the clutch, feeling excited that they would be great to decorate my next event. For those who know me I love hosting wonderful events, so imagine just how excited I was about this gift.

Moments later, my excitement turned into despair as I realized that these "ribbons" weren't ribbons. They were snakes! I dropped them immediately and, in an instant, I found myself killing snakes.

Snakes in a dream represent witchcraft. As I attempted to kill each snake, I found myself smashing their heads and was successful killing all of them.

Almost immediately without leaving the room, I looked out the window and saw a familiar face standing outside who was about to be bitten by another snake. I tried to warn her to move away from the approaching snake, but she wouldn't listen to me. In the end, somehow I grabbed a handful of sand at threw it at the snake, but it formed a sand mountain over both the snake and the individual. I knew at that point that the person's doom was inevitable, as she was now buried under the sand with the snake.

Next in the dream, I'm still looking out the window but it's as if I am now face to face with a giant movie screen. The screen showed the inside of a huge event hall full of people. There was a camera panning the room allowing me to see what was happening inside the room. I saw hundreds of people sitting around looking incredibly sad. As the camera continued to pan the room, it came around to the front of the room where there was a red coffin. When I saw the red coffin, my reaction was: "Oh, she died!" And with that knowledge, the screen disappeared, and I was now (mentally), back inside the apartment. I never left the room physically.

Inside the apartment a familiar face other than my husband popped up. The person said: "Where is (my husband)?" I immediately looked over at the dirty mattress to see that he was no longer laying there. In fact, he had disappeared altogether. I responded: "You're right! Where did he go? He left me here to kill all these snakes by myself."

I immediately said: "I need to get to church." I then looked down at what I was wearing and saw that I was wearing a short, white beach dress. The dress was extremely transparent. I realized I would need something underneath to cover up myself for church. With that understanding I began to search through all the dirty clothes inside the apartment. And with that thought, I remembered I had a black skirt. I began to search through the dirty clothes to find my skirt.

As I searched for my black skirt amongst the mess, I stumbled upon and uncovered a huge, transparent plastic bag with five decapitated snake heads that were being preserved in some type of clear liquid. They were hidden under the dirty clothes. It was evident that the snake heads had been cut off for some time, at least days, because they were losing color and changing to a pale shade of grey, but they still had some life left in them. Their eyes were rolled back but they were still panting for air. It was evident they were on their last breath, but I wanted to make sure I killed them. I grabbed a metal pole close by and began to smash each snake's head to pieces, finishing them off one by one. I continued to search for the black skirt amongst the mess but then I woke up with an urgency, repeating the same words from the dream: "I need to get to church."

I had many questions about the dream. And you are probably wondering why all these details from the dream or even why mention the dream at all. What does the dream have to do with the title of this book? Everything. It will hopefully make sense in a few.

I reached out to a dear friend whom I trusted to help me with the interpretation of the dream. The first thing they shared with me was that the snakes represented witchcraft. The chocolate clutch (purse) I received was brown. He asked me what was significant about the color chocolate brown. I mentioned that it was my favorite color. He said that is an unusual color to have as a favorite color. He said the person who is responsible for the witchcraft knows you very well. The witchcraft you are dealing with is an inside job. The witch knows you well enough to give you something you would like in your favorite color knowing you would easily accept it.

At this point, I realized I was now dealing with a different witch, a second witch. Please remember this thought as it will make sense later.

I cannot describe to you the magnitude of the mental warfare I was experiencing during this time. This was not just about a separation; I was literally warring for my mind especially in the night hours when I should be sleeping. The warfare was intense! I would literally sense demonic presence in my room. It took intense praying and listening to worship music and even listening to others pray online to keep my mind or to help me get much needed sleep.

I had so many questions as nothing around me made sense. I would continue to cry out to the Lord for answers. One morning in prayer as I was desperately seeking the Lord, the Holy Spirit randomly asked me "Who in the Bible was drawn from the water?" My answer was "Moses." This was significant as the Lord brought back to my memory the story of me almost drowning as a baby and like baby Moses, someone had to "draw me out" from the water. The Lord then asked: "Who was Moses?" My response: "A deliverer." The Lord then responded: "And so are you. You both were drawn from the water." I found that to be quite an interesting response, but still, I didn't quite understand what the Lord meant by any of it.

Allow me to pause here to say that God is the greatest scrapbooker ever. He wastes no detail about our lives. Every part of our story is significant, and He intentionally weaves it into our destiny. No matter how we were birthed or whom He used to bring us here, He allowed it because He intended to get the glory out of it. Someone may be saying but you don't understand, I was born out of rape or incest or out of wedlock. God is not surprised or moved by any of those details. He knew how you would get here, and He intended for you to be here, even under unfavorable circumstances. God uses the good, bad and in between to bring glory to His name. How you got here did not disqualify you from being a part of His masterplan. So gentle reminder, your story doesn't stop there. It's not so much about *how* you were born but more so on *why* you were born. There is so much attached to the why than to the how. If you allow Him, He will stitch the beautiful pieces of your quilt into a masterpiece!

While I am here in this moment, I also want to take a moment to release that parent, who's lived the shame of how their child was conceived or birthed. You don't have to be ashamed. An unpleasant situation gave birth to someone beautiful. Someone who God intended from the foundations of the earth to bring glory and honor to His name. Release yourself from the mental anguish and pain, the shame, and accept that God CHOSE you as a part of His great plan and He has every intention to use those parts of your quilt, even the parts you may not be so proud of to bring to pass something great. Out of your pain came something or someone beautiful. Your pain produced purpose! Glory to God. Despite the unfavorable events or circumstances around what and how it happened, God chose to bring into this world a world changer!

Chapter 5:
The GREAT REVEAL

Now back to the story…

During the first few weeks of this warfare, not realizing how intense things would become in the next few months, I was praying steadily for my marriage. As I prayed, one morning I had an encounter with the Lord. Prior to that He would drop little nuggets or questions in my spirit that would cause me to think. When the Lord revealed that I was a deliverer, I needed clarity. I really did not understand the depth of what He meant so He began to take me down a journey.

The Lord spoke to me about a certain individual that I thought didn't like me. He said "The person you think doesn't like you, knows who you are. *YOU* don't know who you are, but she recognized who you are in the spirit the moment you showed up on the scene. She is a witch. And she knows you are a deliverer. She knows you would be the one to come into her bloodline and break curses and expose her!" With this revelation my jaws dropped. I couldn't believe what I was hearing. It now makes sense why she tried everything to break up the marriage. She even boycotted the wedding.

Hosea 4:6 says, "My people are destroyed for lack of knowledge..." The enemy relies on and banks on our ignorance. He uses it as a weapon against us. Because we don't know who we are and understand the authority in which we walk, he uses us as punching bags. But I love how the Lord will ask a question or make a statement that will trigger us and send us on a seek after him to find out the answer. Proverbs 25:2 says, "It is the glory of God to conceal a thing: but the honor of kings is to search out a matter." So, in response to His statement, I went on a quest to uncover what He meant by that statement. "Lord, who am I?"

Days prior I was pondering on something about my childhood. For some reason that week the thought kept coming up over and over and I found myself sharing something with a friend that I had only shared with a handful of people who were close to me.

As a little girl, I was submerged under water and almost drowned. I was drawn from the water by a neighbor who stated that if he had showed up just a few seconds later, I would've drowned. He showed up just in time. For some reason that story was sitting in my spirit along with another incident that occurred when I was about eleven years old.

At eleven years old, I attended school in the town of Mandeville, Manchester which was about a 30-minute commute by car from my home. One evening, as I was preparing to catch a taxi home, I noticed that there was a huge crowd gathered in the center of the town. Out of curiosity, I made my way to see what was taking place. It looked like some type of "revival". Now as a little girl, brought up in church, I understood what a revival was. However, this one looked quite different. Out of curiosity I walked up to the crowd of over a hundred or more people gathered around one individual to see what was happening.

Walking up to the crowd I saw a man dressed in white with his head also wrapped in white cloth. He would call out certain individuals from the crowd and would speak to them about things that would happen to them, but he would also advise them how he could prevent it if they drank this or did some form of ritual he would prescribe for a monetary cost. Folks were lined up with their money ready for him to call them out next to fix whatever it is they were dealing with in their personal lives.

Out of curiosity, I made my way closer to the crowd. As soon as I blended into the crowd, I noticed the man stopped talking and paused his "performance." His back was turned towards me. Suddenly, as if he felt interrupted, he began to turn around slowly. At that point, I noticed the scowl on his face. Next thing I knew he was staring at me angrily, eyeball to eyeball. I became so scared and quickly pulled away from amongst the crowd and walked over towards the other side. He then resumed his activities.

Still out of curiosity, I made my way to the other side of the crowd. As mentioned previously, there was a circle of approximately one hundred or more folks gathered around him. As a curious child I still wanted to see what was happening. After all, wasn't that just a coincidence that he had stopped and stared at me? So, as I inched my way to peek inside the crowd, I was careful not to reveal my entire body. I just wanted a small opening behind the crowd enough where my eyes could peek through without being noticed.

As I peeked through a little opening in the crowd, I noticed something familiar. Once again, the man stopped his activities and with his back turned he began to walk over towards the direction where I was. Coincidence? Moments later he stopped right in front of where I was. But he couldn't see me, I thought. Almost immediately he ducked down to where my eyes were with that same angry scowl as if to say, "beat it!" I was so scared I took off running.

That incident plagued me for many years. I only shared it a few years ago, some 30+ years later, when a family member shared with me about an encounter she had at work where a palm reader showed up. She said the palm reader was reading everyone's palm for free, and she waited to go last. She was excited to find out what the palm reader would say concerning her. As it her turn came to go next, she said the palm reader took one look at her and almost dropped the cards and started to hurry out the door screaming, "Get away from me! I can't touch you! You're one of them! You're marked!" As I heard her story, I became curious because I realized then that perhaps I was "marked" too! Still there were no answers for what "marked" meant or why both those incidences occurred.

Now to go back to the encounter I had during prayer time at the time of this warfare I had going on in my marriage. These incidents kept coming up in my thoughts and I found it strange that as I was praying for restoration, the Lord would instead remind me of these strange encounters that happened years ago. I kept asking the Lord to help me understand and answer the questions I had been asking all this time and show me how they're connected to my current situation. And let me tell you something, He did! Glory to God!

The Lord began to share with me that the man from my childhood in the park who was operating under demonic influence recognized who I was. He knew you were called to be a deliverer. That's why he was uncomfortable performing his rituals in front of you.

The demons in the person who opposed your marriage

knew who you are and that you have been sent into that bloodline to expose her for who she was, a witch. Her demons understood you were sent in the bloodline because you had an assignment. They knew if they didn't stop you, you would cancel out the bloodline curses that plagued that family. What's interesting to note, is that the person may or may not know why they don't like you or what it is about you why their spirit isn't connecting with you but the demons in them knows quite well that they can't afford for you to show up and cancel out their assignment.

Now, I know this is some heavy stuff. Trust me, I felt like a bomb dropped on me, but I wanted to make sense of it all. With each new revelation it opened me up to ask even more questions. What did all this have to do with my husband and the warfare I was in? Everything!

It was then the Lord said: "I had to allow you to experience what you're going through so you can get delivered in it, so that you can discover the tools you have to cancel out the assignments of the enemy working against you and those connected to you. When you truly understand who you are and your "why", I can then use you to deliver others". Like adult Moses, I had to re-learn my true identity. A lot of things were starting to come full circle.

We are talking about the power of the altar. Notice that every question I had was answered on the altar, in prayer. Revelation came from my place and time spent on the altar. Insight came from the altar. It was on the altar that my purpose was unleashed.

Now back to the witch. I've been using this term and have yet given definition of who a witch is. It's a term we use loosely when we don't care too much for an individual that might have a nasty demeanor. But a witch is more than that. The term too is often misused out of context. So, to be fair let's explore this whole concept of a witches and witchcraft. Let's bring definitions and clarity to substantiate statements that are being made.

As mentioned previously, my intentions are not to destroy people's reputations but to destroy the secrets, schemes and altars of the enemy. If any of Satan's agents become identifiable throughout this book, then my only hope is that they take the time to repent, there's yet room on the altar. We can't patty cake with the enemy and the folks he's using to come against the people, plan and purpose of God.

So, the basic definition of a witch is, anyone who uses sneaky tactics or extreme force to control or manipulate another person to do what they want them to do, which is usually opposite of what that person wants to do or what God's plan is for their life. They try to divert the plan of God in that individual's life. They try to "make it happen" for that individual because they themselves want personal gain from the outcome of the situation.

Personal gain could be the satisfaction of bullying the person and getting what they want aka a power trip. Or it could be tangible goods that would benefit the witch. They may, like in my case, oppose a marriage because they don't think that person is right for you. Or they may feel as though with a spouse present, they will no longer have control over you and will no longer be able to manipulate you. They may oppose the church you attend or where you work. They will try to control every decision you make. You must do things their way or else.

Witches operate under the influence of fallen angels, otherwise known as demons. These demons were once angels who lived in the presence of God where the glory is. They experienced His presence, but because of rebellion, they permanently lost their place in heaven and can never get back to glory. They are drawn to believers, but especially ones who exhibit a strong presence of the anointing operating in his/her life.

Demons operating in a witch, recognizes the glory of God manifesting in a person's life and will send the witch to connect with that person. The witch will try to live vicariously through that individual. They show up and attach to weaker, unsuspecting, but anointed vessels trying to manipulate the glory. The bigger problem is that at some point they will turn on the victim and destroy their anointing and eventually the individual.

Witches are folks who are always trying to make it happen in their own strength without the glory of God. They want to ascend to the top without the process. They want their own glory instead of giving God the glory. They recognize that they, themselves have no anointing, so they attach themselves to a believer to try to manipulate the glory on the believer's life to get what they want. They want titles and accolades. They want power for personal gain, and they want it without process. By now you've probably guessed it, witches do operate under a strong influence of the spirit of pride and rebellion and they show up with an agenda.

Oh, these witches appear sweet and kind, innocent and soft spoken until you make them angry. This is why sometimes it can be hard to detect a witch. But make them angry enough and they will fly into a rage or temper tantrum. Witches become incredibly angry when they are exposed, or they feel they can no longer control or manipulate you.

Witches are identifiable by their need to control people and situations. They are not in charge, but they need to supersede or oppose whoever is in charge. They have the spirit of Lucifer who held a high-ranking position next to the leader, (God), but is never satisfied until they try to overrule and overtake the leader. That's why when they are identified they must be exposed immediately. It's their demise or yours!

Because they are subtle you won't notice right away that they are controlling or manipulating. They are your right-hand person, your confidant, the person who has your back. They have a Jezebel spirit that wants to fulfill your every desire and get you what you want. They want to do everything for you, so you become dependent upon them. You rely on them for everything, so much that you no longer pray or believe God by faith because you know they are going to step in and fix it for you.

The longer you are around a witch, the further away from the altar you become. Yes, you may still pray but your prayers are nothing but sounding brass and tinkling symbols. There is no faith attached to your prayer. Your agenda to serve God pure heartedly is now twisted and tainted as you're not operating under demonic influence and interference. Your service now becomes performance.

Witches must always have things their way. If they cannot control you, they will stop at nothing to manipulate. They manipulate by buying you gifts, offering you large sums of money, volunteering while tearing up the other volunteers. They will meet your every want or need, or by being your best help. Witches like to be needed, which is half the problem. They want to become your source or resource, so you are totally dependent on them. If that's not feasible, they will be your best confidant. You unknowingly are feeding all your information to them which makes it easy for them to work against you. It's like taking candy from a baby. And that my friend is serious stuff.

At the core of a witch is someone who once experienced serious rejection and has now decided they will control everyone and everything around them so they will never experience that form of rejection again. This spirit of rejection opened up a portal through which other demons entered, and are now operating as a legion, (group of demons) in a person.

Now, you may be wondering, how does one become a witch. Some witches are born, which means they themselves entered into some demonic covenant or agreements and is the first of their kind in their family's bloodline. Others inherit their "powers" through bloodline curses or transfers. Those are the witches who were initiated by other witches within their family or circle. For example, if a witch is dying, she could pass her "powers" down to another person in the family to continue the wickedness.

Stick with me, I know this is a lot. Imagine what I went through in the past year of "classroom time" learning all this firsthand. The best analogy I could give is that it's like not knowing how to swim and then being tossed into the middle of the rough ocean with only a life vest, only to discover that it was a life and death moment, and I had no choice but to learn how to swim right then and there to save my life or drown! The good news is that I went through the hard part to help you, so you wouldn't have to.

So, to go back to that family witch previously mentioned. That individual boycotted our wedding and from day one would sow many seeds of discord to cause friction in my marriage. She wanted nothing to do with me and refused to accept that I was now my husband's spouse.

During this time of revelation, I could not even begin to tell you in mere words what this period was like. I was learning some things about me, discovering the magnitude of jealous "friends" around me, fighting witchcraft and witches, missing my husband, showing up at work, managing home responsibilities, dealing with gossip and still had to maintain my kingdom assignments as best as I could.

It was only by the grace of God that I did not lose my mind. I could literally sense the demonic presence and activities around me. It was intense! I thank God for the prayers of the few that cared enough to pray for and check up on me constantly.

About a week later, on a Sunday morning, I was praying and heard Holy Spirit tell me to reach out to one of my cousins in Jamaica and ask her to pray for me. I had not spoken to my cousin at this time for over a month or so and I didn't want to reach out to her because I wanted to keep what was happening to myself. My cousin is trustworthy to keep my business protected and is indeed a powerful Intercessor, but I just didn't want to share what I was going through just yet. So, in total disobedience I did not reach out.

The very next Monday morning, exactly one week after I had had the dream I discussed previously, I received an inbox from that same cousin. The inbox said, "Hey Cuz how are you?" My response was: "Hey Cuz I'm doing ok." As I responded I clearly heard Holy Spirit say stop lying and tell her the truth. So, with conviction

I replied "Actually no I am not ok. I am going through something." She then called me and said: "Let me tell you what you are going through. This morning Holy Spirit woke me up to pray at 5am and showed me that you are going through a battle concerning your marriage and ministry." She said: "The Lord showed me a witch that has come up against your marriage and your ministry. But the Bible says suffer not a witch to live!"I began to weep and was able to come clean and confirm everything she said to me. I also shared with her how Holy Spirit directed me to call her, and I was disobedient. But how He woke her up to show her what I wouldn't share.

How powerful and personal is our God! He fights for us, and He is concerned about everything that concerns us!

Later that same day, I received a phone call from a friend of mine from Pennsylvania. This particular friend and her husband pastors a church in PA. They were in the middle of a 40 day fast and would have prayer at 6pm daily. That day, they had a special guest intercessor on the phone line. This man of God did not know I existed. As he was praying, he picked me up in the spirit. Keep in mind, I was in NY at the time and was not on the prayer line. I had no idea they were having prayer.

So, the man of God picks me up in the spirit and calls me by name. He asked if they knew someone by the name "Nadine." They confirmed they did. He said: "She is either a pastor or minister. Do you know her?" They confirmed they knew who I was. He said: "Her marriage and ministry are under attack. There is a witch that brought something into her home."He then quoted the same scripture my cousin quoted "suffer not a witch to live."

Now, if you lost count let me help you, by this time I am now dealing with witch number three. The previous two witches had never been in my home. This third witch brought something into my home. Now, I can count on one hand the few individuals that visited my home. Which one of those individuals is the witch?

Only folks close to me are permitted into my home. I am a "homebody" and don't really have a lot of foot traffic in my home. Only a few folks have been to my residency or even know where I live. So, trying to figure out or accept revelation of who this could be was a thought I wrestled with.

Now at this point in the story, I know this all sounds outrageous, but I want you to understand that the enemy's greatest weapon in this hour is the spirit of deception. If he can have you to believe none of this is true, then he has already won. As I stated, prior to this experience and the writing of this book, I was one of the ones who was deceived by being naïve to the wiles and devices of the enemy. I was super trusting and that gave room for the enemy to pull wool over my eyes, for far too long.

God is calling us to wake up from our slumber! The Bible says in Ephesians 6:12, "For we wrestle not against flesh and blood, but against principalities, against powers, against the rulers of the darkness of this world, against spiritual wickedness in high places." We are so busy fighting individuals when there are spirits behind the scenes manipulating these people against us. And the sad part is, that sometimes these folks don't even know that they are being used and manipulated by the enemy! If you were to confront them, they would be offended and deny any of this because they themselves sometimes don't recognize that they are the catalyst the enemy is using to destroy someone else's life.

Another fact is that the folks warring against you or being used are not your obvious enemies! Yes, you can identify folks who are obviously jealous of you, who don't like you, but can I tell you… as subtle and cunning as Satan is, he is not using the folks that you would suspect. He will not use the obvious representatives. Instead, he chooses to use unsuspecting folks very close to you because of course that's what makes the attack so effective.   He will use your friends, your spouse and sometimes close family members, (as mentioned previously, sometimes even unbeknownst to them that they are being used).

They are close enough to see your failures but are secretly jealous of what they deem to be your successes. Some are being used because they live vicariously through you, so they manipulate their way to get you to do their bidding. The scary part is that they are so close and because you trust them, you can't see the damage they are causing. They are in your face smiling with a knife in your back! For this next dimension of your life/ministry, pray for discernment. You will absolutely need a greater measure of discernment, or you will be deceived in this hour.

CHAPTER 6:
IS IT MENTAL HEALTH (PSYCHOSIS) OR DEMONS?

Now, I know I might still have you in skepticism about this whole demonic and witchcraft stuff. So, before I go any further let's address this using scripture. Please keep in mind that my assignment is not to try to convince you per se, but more so to give you enough information to open up your spiritual eyes to the deception and devices of the enemy.

In Luke Chapter 4:33-36 Jesus shows up at the Synagogue. While He's there "a man with a demon" was present:

"And in the synagogue, there was a man, which had a spirit of an unclean devil, and cried out with a loud voice, saying, let us alone; what have we to do with thee, thou Jesus of Nazareth? art thou come to destroy us? I know thee who thou art; the Holy One of God. And Jesus rebuked him, saying, hold thy peace, and come out of him. And when the devil had thrown him in the midst, he came out of him and hurt him not. And they were all amazed, and spake among themselves, saying, whata word is this! for with authority and power he commandeth the unclean spirits, and they come out."

We are living in a day when there havebeen medical breakthroughs, medical terminologies that almost conflict with the Bible. For example, we just read in the scripture where a man had a demon, but in today's world, we would say he had some form of psychosis or mental health disorder. I can even imagine someone reading this may even say that my writing is based on me experiencing a great deal of trauma during my separation and that I'm experiencing some form of psychosis as this is my brain's way of coping with the stress. I beg to differ. So, let's look at the word "psychosis".

Psy·cho·sis

A severe mental condition in which thought and emotions are so affected that contact is lost with external reality.

Medical terminologies used today are often not mentioned in the Bible. So, this leaves many questioning or uncertain of what is actually taking place or the best way to identify or approach these type situations they may be facing.

So, am I dealing with a mental health disorder or am I dealing with a demon? Or am I dealing with both? As a sidebar, as I'm typing this portion of the book I'm sitting on the train and there are currently two such individuals manifesting via loud outbursts on the train. Coincidence? Could be, but for some reason, I don't think so!

So, is it demonic activity or mental illness? Are they two different things? Is one being influenced by the other? And if we are asking these questions there are other questions we might as well ask. Are demons even real and if they are, how do I know when it's a mental illness vs a demon in operation? We may even go as far as asking, can someone who is a believer be oppressed or possessed by a demon? And the list of questions/concerns goes on and on.

So, when seeking answers the response varies depending on who is responding and their level of experience with either or both. Perhaps, if you ask a therapist/psychologist or other medical professional, chances are you will get a medical response such as, "According to the DSM… he/she is showing signs of…", and some form of psychosis would probably be named. If we asked a non-medical, blood bought believer chances are you may hear it's a demon. And sometimes you will hear from either that it's a bit of both.

So, depending on whom you're speaking to the answer will vary. Which makes it easy and reasonable to struggle with uncertainty. Someone may ask themselves, am I too zealous spiritually to think it's a demon when it's a diagnosis that can be treated medically?

Let's peer deeper into the text as I want to attempt to bring some clarity to these questions we may have. As we just read, in Luke 4, this man was in the synagogue. So, would it be fair to safely say he was in a place equivalent to being in the church? Hope we can agree on that.

Notice where he was. He was in the synagogue (or church) amongst the believers. Was he already exhibiting signs of demonic behavior when he walked through the doors or was it that he showed up to church and began manifesting? We are not sure as to some details but what we do know is that he was in the synagogue when Jesus noticed him showing signs of "having a demon." It didn't say he was possessed by it. The verse said he "had" a demon. There is a difference.

So, what is the difference between having a demon and being possessed by a demon? Having a demon is that there is a demon oppressing the individual. To be oppressed means to be controlled by. You can be controlled from the inside or outside much like a puppet.

Possessed means to own something or have complete power over it. It would mean then that one is owned by a demon, or the demon has complete power over that individual. For example, if I buy a piece of land, I now own it. So, at the time of ownership I take (full) possession of the land. I now have legal rights owning the property. So, in a case where a person is demon possessed, it would mean that the demon owns or has full control of the individual.

If the demon had complete power over the person, it could do whatever it wanted. If a demon has complete power over a person, they could and likely would kill that person. The Bible says the enemy comes to kill, steal and destroy. If he has full power over an individual, especially a believer he would do everything in his power to kill that person. Killing that believer would snuff out their God-given purpose and derail the plan God has for their lives. You need to understand that your purpose affects nations and generations, so if the enemy were to have his way with you, he would snuff you out before it materialized and affected so many. The enemy is not that powerful.

Believers are not owned by demons, but we can be influenced by demons via oppression from the outside or by having an evil spirit enter inside of us via legal access that we permit. We will talk more about how this happens.

"Having a demon" is like a laptop that has a virus. The laptop is not owned by the virus but there is interference. Dangerous interference that can wipe out the software. When a virus is detected, it must be wiped out immediately by anti-virus software or it will cause major damage to the host. It can seem like the virus has full control over your device, but it doesn't. But the longer the virus stays the more dangerous it becomes and the more damage it causes.

I know this may seem as if I'm belaboring the point, but I hope to make this as bite-sized and as clear as possible. So, let's look at one more example. Covid is a virus. When someone contracted the virus, it entered our bodies wreaking havoc, yet we were not possessed by the virus. We just knew that it was in our system causing internal damage and we needed to get rid of it before it resulted in the host's fatality, caused from the damages done to major organs. Please know that the longer a demon stays inside of a person, the more damage it will cause to the individual and to others who come in contact with that individual.

So, the question remains, can a demon possess a believer? What can you deduct from all this information provided? I am going to leave the deduction up to you. I will not try to convince you either way. Pray and ask Holy Spirit for clarity.

As folks living on this side of the world known as the "western world," we are prone to be more "modernized," leaving us to be more scientific than spiritual. We tend to not believe in demons and witches because we have alternative suggestions or information that provide "solutions" to almost any given situation we come up against. But if we lived in places where spiritual warfare and demons are prevalent like Africa, the Caribbean islands etc., we would beg to differ. Here in the western world, we medicate a lot of people exhibiting signs of demonic activity. In third world countries, folks who don't have the medical resources we have, find other ways to deal with these spirits. Some believers in those countries understand in most cases the only "cure" is to cast those evil spirits out in the name of Jesus!

Some time ago, I was in Jamaica with some friends praying for a friend who had a terminal illness in her body. As we prayed, demons began to manifest. The chief demon spoke out of the individual and told us that he was responsible for the illness she had . He began to tell us details of how she became ill, who the witches were behind the illness and shared with us the instructions he had and how he planned to destroy her body to bring about her fatality.

As we laid hands on her to pray, we would touch specific areas in her body and the demon would scream: "Don't touch me!" The demon was sitting where the sickness existed in the person's body. The person had a mass that blocked the individual from going to the bathroom on her own. When we cast out the demon, she called us the next morning to tell us that for the first time in a long time she was able to relieve herself and kept going the entire night. When the demon left, the mass also disappeared!

After that experience, I had a better understanding of sickness and how they are powered by demons seated in that area of the person's body. I shared that story to say, yes infirmities and mental health conditions do exist, but there is a spirit behind those conditions driving it. If I didn't believe this prior, I do now, after having that face-to-face conversation with that foul spirit. The enemy wants us to limit the existence of these conditions to just a physical, chemical or neurological disorder, but I want to highlight that there is also a spiritual component that needs to be addressed.

CHAPTER 7:
HOW SIN GIVES ACCESS TO DEMONIC ACTIVITIES

When dealing with the spiritual component or demonic activities affecting us today, we must address sin and the role it plays in all of this. "Let no man say when he is tempted, I am tempted of God: for God cannot be tempted with evil, neither he any man. But every man is tempted, when he is drawn away of his own lust, and is enticed. Then, when lust hath conceived, it bringeth forth sin: and sin, when it is finished, bringeth forth death." James 1:1-15. It is very clear in scripture that our own desires birth sin.

So where are those desires coming from? They are influenced by demonic oppression. It's important to note that the enemy can plant thoughts into our minds. We also, if we do not guard our gates will begin to lust after what seems pleasurable, giving birth to sin.

How is that possible if the Greater One lives on the inside of us that we can still sin? Simply that, as long as we still live in a body wrapped in flesh, we will always be tempted to sin. Our flesh loves and enjoys pleasure and sin is pleasurable (Hebrew 11:25).

The flesh is always warring against the spirit trying to fulfill the desires of the flesh. These carnal desires oppose the will of God.

The enemy banks in on our proclivity to sin as he understands that sin is a portal or entry way for demonic activity. Our flesh must be subdued. When it's not, it tries hard to rule us, giving access to seducing spirits and driving us away from the will of God for our lives. This is why it is important to repent daily so that we can erase anything that may give the enemy room or access in our lives.

So going back to the dream I had. I began to watch as each piece of the dream began to unfold. I was surprised at the details and clarity and who was being used. As I watched in bewilderment, I continued to pray and follow the instructions of the Lord.

Remembering how filthy my home was in the dream and hearing what the prophet said that the witch had brought something into my home, I knew I had to get my home in order. It wasn't that my place was physically dirty, but the atmosphere had become contaminated. I had to shut down my home to cleanse the atmosphere.

In the dream my home was dirty and chaotic because something was off in the atmosphere. Because the atmosphere was contaminated, it was now a breeding ground for demonic activity which caused confusion and chaos, blocking prayers from being answered. No wonder I was experiencing so much warfare in my marriage.

Let me also state that a person that is dabbling with witchcraft may not be doing things to you directly, but because unclean spirits are attached to them, those spirits can indirectly affect you when they are in your space. It is important to guard your sacred space. Not everyone should have access to your home. Be careful who you eat from or who gives you special gifts.

I know it sounds so ridiculous that one needs to be so cautious of everyone and everything. All I'm going to say is you can heed the warning of someone else's experience, or you can have your own experience with it. Remember, we wrestle not against flesh and blood. And there is an enemy that is waging war against your soul. He's not playing fair. He has a plan to wipe you out any chance he gets, at any cost, because you are no longer a part of his dark kingdom.

I realized not only did I have to shut down my home, but I needed to shut my mouth as well. As young girls we have best friends and people we confide in. We go all the way back to pajama parties and sleepovers, But, as adults, we must mature beyond that place realizing that people change and so do we. We shouldn't be so trusting, sharing everything with everyone because they have always been there in our lives. Overtime folks learn to envy and covet what you have. Some will find themselves competing with you, while you are just simply trying to obey God, not looking for any clout.

Because a witch's nature is that of a controlling manipulating spirit, they often use divination to gain knowledge or hidden information on their subjects or victims. Witches tend to be folks with monitoring spirits. They stay close enough to their unsuspecting victim wanting to know every detail about a person and will monitor and study them to decipher their future in order to abort their destiny. They are used to you feeding them information. It's like taking candy from a baby.

Remember Naboth, in 1Kings 21? It was his neighbor who coveted what he had and because he wouldn't give them what rightfully belonged to him, they killed him. They were willing to take his life to have what he had. Envy is a wicked spirit that will cause one to commit murder to get what it wants. Naboath's death came because of his neighbors, Ahab and Jezebel, who lived in close proximity to him, for years. I'm sure they shared many "good mornings" and saw him working hard to maintain what he had. They couldn't care less about what it took for him to get that vineyard much less maintain it or what it meant to him to keep it and may be one day pass it down in his family to the next generation. All they cared about was what they wanted, and they would stop at nothing to get it. Even if it meant taking his life.

CHAPTER 8:
WITCHCRAFT, NARCISSISM AND DIVINATION

The spirits of Jezebel and Ahab are examples of narcissistic spirits. A narcissist is extremely selfish and self-centered and has an exaggerated view of their own self-importance. They are not people centered, meaning they lack deep emotional connections or empathy. Narcissists are obsessed with their own personal gain and will use whoever is available to get what they want.

Ahab and Jezebel represents two types of narcissists who work interchangeably together: the covert and overt narcissists. Ahab spirit is that of the covert narcissist who uses manipulation to get what he wants. He plays the frustrated, highly depressed, sulking type of individual, hoping someone will have pity on him to give him what he wants. He's the type of narcissist that throws a rock and hides his hands, pretending to be the victim. It is a sneaky spirit but extremely wicked spirit.

Jezebel is representative of the overt narcissist. This type of narcissist is the opposite of, but complimentary to the covert. It is bold, fearless and shameless. It will stop at nothing to get what it wants. It is a people-pleasing spirit that likes to "make it happen" for others in order to gain their favor.

Narcissists will destroy people close to them or a far off with no remorse. This includes spouse, children, friends, leaders. They usually are found close to leaders because they secretly envy them and wants their notoriety, power and resources. This spirit is rooted in individuals who struggle with the spirit of rejection and insecurity. It is a very prideful spirit that does not honor the spirit of the Lord. It will use whatever means necessary for personal gain, including the pulpit. This spirit seeks power and prominence and wants to be worshiped. It wants to take the place of God. Sounds familiar? We can trace this spirit to that old serpent, Lucifer who wanted to ascend and make himself like God, (Exodus 14:13-14). The spirit of divination powers this spirit.

DIVINATION comes from the Greek word "PUTON" which is translated "PYTHON", python as in snake. Isn't that something? Witches are narcissistic. Narcissists are powered by divination. Divination is translated as python or snake. And where did we first see the snake?

He first made his debut in Genesis chapter 3, where he beguiled Eve, in the Garden of Eden. Its deceptive spirit traces back to Satan, the master deceiver.   Because of his deception beguiling Eve, a portal or entryway was opened, giving access for sin to enter humanity, which ultimately leads to natural and spiritual death.

Divination is used to gain knowledge, power and control from a demonic source. This is not a coincidence that in my dream mentioned earlier I was killing snakes. I was dealing with the spirit of divination associated with witchcraft.

The root word for divination is divine, in Latin "divinare". In Greek,the word for divine is mantis, which means prophets. The enemy imitates and perverts everything the Lord does so therefore the diviners or those who practice divination are evil prophets/seers. Their source providing information is demonic. Without discernment it is difficult to tell whether they're a true prophet or just someone working for a profit. You will catch that later. So, don't be surprised if the witch can foretell certain things happening around you. They may try to tell you that God said this or that but the source is not God. It is divination at work.

Do you remember when Saul wanted to know what would be the outcome of Israel's battle against the Philistines (1 Samuel 28)? He once had the true Prophet, Samuel, giving him counsel. But now with Samuel deceased, Saul went to pray to the Lord concerning what he should do next. The Lord did not answer him. So, feeling restless and overwhelmed, Samuel decided to take matters into his own hands to consult with a witch, specifically the witch of Endor. He disguised himself as he went to see her, as he did not want anyone to recognize him. He himself, had banned all witches and mediums but now when pressure arose, he was desperate for information, so he sought out a one-on-one consultation. When pressure arise in the lives of some believers, if they are not careful to seek the Lord and rest in Him until the answer comes, they could find themselves giving heed to seducing spirits.

Folks dabble with divination because they want fast answers. We live in an internet sensation generation where folks want everything at their fingertips. It's an "I want to know now", itchy ears generation.

Even in church we have prophetic junkies. Folks who will not show up for prayer meetings, nor participate in worship. They will fall asleep during the preached word but will actively participate and be alert only when it's time for the prophetic word. They will travel across the country for a prophetic word from their favorite prophet but not walk a block for a prayer meeting.

The Bible says in 2 Timothy 4:3-4, "For the time is coming when people will not endure sound teaching but having itching ears they will accumulate for themselves teachers to suit their own passions and will turn away from listening to the truth and wander off into myths".

We must be so careful with being prophetically hungry that we allow ourselves to feed off folks who operate under the spirit of divination. Folks who are leading and because of the pull from those following, they now feel the need to perform or to give the people what they crave the most, prophesies to keep membership.

There are so many prophets that have popped up out of nowhere these days. They mostly prophesy material gain but hardly ever point us to true repentance and back to the altar. Rarely these days, do you hear a prophet, in a time when people have become so perverse, correcting or rebuking the Body of Christ? This is dangerous!

Divination is the "spirit of python" or the "spirit of the snake." We know a snake is also referred to as a serpent and we remember the spirit of the serpent very well as he first made his debut in Genesis where he beguiled Eve. So, we can safely trace the spirit of divination back to that same ole serpent, satan.

Now, I know you may be challenged with the thought of how a diviner can be influenced by Satan if the information provided seem so accurate, when he is the father of lies. If satan is a liar how is it that the information provided is true? If you have ever had an up-close encounter with a demon, when you speak to them, they must respond by telling the truth. This is because we have authority over them, so they are forced to submit to the greater authority and respond accordingly. However, this is true when we are confronting them directly.

However, when they are influencing someone, they rely on their ability to deceive you by manipulating the facts. Remember in Genesis 3, the enemy subtly questioned Eve about what she knew to be true. He wanted her to second guess the instructions given by the Lord previously. Once he was able to plant doubt in her mind or there was an opening to consider an alternative meaning to what was already stated, he then went in for the guzzler and twisted the facts, re-presenting them to her in a way that appealed to her intellect.

It is extremely dangerous to engage your intellect to consult with what your spirit man knows to be true. When the Lord speaks, by faith we should receive the word even if it conflicts with what (we think) we know to be facts. Don't let your mind, influenced by the enemy, to talk you out of what God has spoken. His words are always true and irrevocable. His words bring life and always have your best interest at heart.

Remember, the enemy is a deceiver so he will lace the truth with lies but make it sound appealing to your ears. All he wants is to bait you enough so he can get a hook in you. Once he gets that hook, his goal is to pull you completely out of the plan and will of God. He will attempt to destroy you by any means necessary! Remember his goal in the life of the believer is to steal, kill and destroy, (John 10:10).

Have you ever considered how a snake kills its victim? It wraps around its prey and squeezes the life out of them, or it swallows them headfirst causing them to suffocate as they are being swallowed.

The spirit of the python likes to be associated with leadership. It stays remarkably close to the leader or whoever has authority/power. If it can mislead or misinform or manipulate the leader, its job is already done. A tainted leader or one being influenced by the spirit of divination will transfer that spirit throughout the group/congregation.

The python spirit will always want to "prophesy". There will be little word, little worship but tons of prophecy. It will be a fast-growing congregation full of itchy ears and prophetic junkies sitting under the spirit of divination and not even knowing it! Lord, help us in this hour to be able to discern which spirit is in operation!

This is why it's important to have a strong Bible based, praying church. There is a need to re-build the altars in the house of God. How do I know there is a strong altar in the house of God where I worship? When you have a strong personal altar unto the Lord your spirit will connect with it. You will also be able to identify the presence of other altars. You will be able to discern that this is not it, or this truly is it.

There was a time when I was a little girl, and I remember being in prayer service where we would be asked at the altar where we would kneel to pray. Even as young children we were able to identify the space designated as the altar in the church. Today, we don't even have altars in some churches anymore or they are not identifiable. We have a praise and worship section, space for the band and the pulpit, but no designated place for prayer. Why do you think some churches are in the state they're in? They have become performance driven. We have plenty of events but no prayer meetings. We are super prophetic but have no prayer life. How are you speaking for God when you haven't even spoken to God? Selah.

The expression still stands: "No prayer, no power. Little prayer, little power. Much prayer, much power." It's time for the altars in our churches to be resuscitated and resurrected. It's time to remove the ashes and light a fresh fire and let it burn. If we want to see revivals breakout all over this nation, if we want to see souls saved and delivered for real, if we want to see miracles signs and wonders then we need to set the altar ablaze. We need to set our altars on fire with our prayers. Only then will we be able to counteract the demonic altars that are being powered by the spirit of divination.

CHAPTER 9:
UNDERSTANDING HOW THESE EVIL SPIRITS WORK AGAINST YOU

Isaiah 61:1, "The Spirit of the Lord God is upon me, because the Lord has anointed me to bring good news to the poor; he has sent me to bind up the brokenhearted, to proclaim liberty to the captives, and the opening of the prison to those who are bound"

At birth, there are angels assigned to you to protect you and to assist you in fulfilling your God-given assessment. In the same way, the enemy also assigns demonic spirits to you, to frustrate your purpose. These demons are assignment specific. So, for example, because I have a deliverance ministry, it will attract folks that need deliverance. It will also attract an unusual amount of personal attacks from the enemy. The attacks are sent to frustrate me and stop me and throw me off so I am not able to meet the need of those individuals. If I am bombarded with personal problems, it will distract me from serving others. This is nothing but tactics the enemy uses.

I know this all sounds like a lot but remind yourself that you are fully equipped for the challenges that comes with the assignment. If He's brought you to it, He will not only see you through but He's already has already assigned angels to assist you. There's no need to fear, Satan is a defeated foe and heaven is backing you!

In the spirit world, as you grow in Christ you will experience new dimensions and new territories. Attacks will come with each dimension you travel. The higher the dimension, the bigger the demon. The greater the territory the greater the influence. The greater your influence as you grow in Christ, the more you will attract demonic activity. Hell is not just going to sit back and admire you as you grow in power and influence to destroy the works of the enemy. Oh, there is going to be great interference strategically to stop you before you even discover your identity, and before you can become effective in your role. But no worries, you are built for this!

A clear sign you are about to be promoted in the spirit is that you will go through one a season of testing. That test will be sent to see if you are ready for your next dimension in your walk with the Lord. Satan will launch his best demons to try to derail you so and try to stop you from passing that test. During the test, do not get weary. That's the time to put on your spiritual armor and locate your altar. Stay there and fight in prayer. As you pray, angels are on assignment fighting for you.

Your test will come from your weakest area in that moment. If you have a lustful spirit like that of Samson or Solomon, he will send you someone attractive as a distraction. If you are a Joseph called to save your generation, he will set family/close friends against you. The very ones you are called to preserve. If you are an Ahab (a weak leader) he will send a Jezebel to partner with you. If your weakness is money, he will send money from the wrong source.

If there are certain proclivities in your family, take note. Those same spirits will come after you especially if they know you are the one chosen to break the family curses. They will try to break you before you break them. For example, anti-marital forces will wage war against your marriage. The Spirit of infirmity will attack your body. Your mental health will come under attack. But let me remind you that you are more than a conqueror and you are fully equipped to overcome these forces and break the generational cycles in your bloodline. Tell that bloodline curse that kept running through your bloodline that it just ran into the wrong one. The issues in my bloodline stop with me. You must be determined to be the one to break those demonic altars so that the residue does not get passed down to your children and your children's children.

CHAPTER 10:
DEMONS, PORTALS, COVENANT AND ALTARS

So far, we have been talking about demons, portals, covenants and even altars. But let's bring definition to each, bringing more clarity to what each is all about.

The word of God says that "my people are destroyed for lack of knowledge" (Hosea 4:6). We cannot rely on assumptions to get us through spiritual warfare. The enemy would only have a field day tearing us up. The more information we have the greater our knowledge, which means the more ammunition we will have, so we can be better armed to fight.

Demons:

Demons are displaced, evil, supernatural beings or entities who seek to gain legal entry into the earth realm via a host or body, which can house and give them access, to influence human affairs. Demons are like squatters; they have no power of ownership, but they understand their legal right according to laws that are in place, which allows them free access to dwell there. Their host granted them free access in the first place because the place was left unkept and unguarded. Now that they have access, because they understand the spiritual laws better than the owner of the house, they will put up a fight to maintain their right to occupy that space. While they are in the house they will wreak havoc and only cause destruction to the host.

While these imps have no real power, they know how to manipulate their host to carry out wicked assignments from Satan against their said victims and against others. Their plan is to go against the will or plan of God for that individual's life or for humanity on a whole. They show up in the individual's life to prevent them from being the vessel God has designed them to be. They gravitate especially to individuals who have influence, who are able to affect the lives of others. If they feel like you can impact others they will try to use you to cause major damage in the earth. If they cannot stop your God-given purpose, then their assignment is to frustrate your purpose and to cause you to forfeit what God has called you to do.

Their tactics may be to influence a musician to write hateful lyrics influencing large groups of people to incite hate on a certain culture. Or they may use a cultist to influence large groups of people to practice a false religion. Their acts are carried out in such a subtle way that at first it seems so innocent, you won't even notice the harm or see the damage that is being done until it's too late.

Demonic influence enters through sin, through trauma (especially childhood trauma), via one's insecurities or perverted habits, through curses or via occultic practices. These spirits enter a person's life through portals or entryways and are always looking for an opportunity to increase their influence. The sad thing is when they gain entry, they usually do not travel alone. They travel with "friend demons" or will later on attract other spirits and invite them to dwell in the host. For example, the spirit of rejection usually travels with the spirit of anger and insecurity and may later on pick up the spirit of envy and jealousy. These demons can dwell together with numerous demons, known as legions.

Demons can oppress one from outside their bodies or from within. We must be so guarded and submitted to the Holy Spirit, abstaining from sin and repenting daily to ensure we are not opening portals giving access to demonic activity in our lives. When we recognize open doors in our lives that gives the enemy access, we must close them right away.

Portals:

Portals are gateways or points of entry where these demons form "covenants" or agreements with their host, knowingly or unknowingly to that individual. The space where this covenant is made is called an altar which is now erected to carry out the function of the covenant.

As mentioned previously, portals are access points or entryways for demonic activity. Demons are traveling back and forth from the spirit world into the natural world constantly. They find ways to enter the natural realm to influence humanity to carry out evil tasks.

Portals or points of access for demonic activity, can be, but are not limited to dreams, covenants/agreements, bloodline curses, perverse behaviors such as sex outside of marriage etc. They enter through our gates. This is why it's so important that we guard our gates. I'll list a few here and give examples.

Your eyes: The eyes are the window to your soul. What you take in visually can affect the conditions of your heart. Be careful to guard your eye gate as demons can enter through electronic screens: television, laptops, phones etc. These are portals that the enemy uses to gain access.

Your ears: What you hear goes into your spirit. Do not allow every and anyone to pour junk into your ears. In John 6:63, Jesus said, "…the words that I speak to you, they are spirit and they are life." We can then assume that the words the enemy speak is also spirit that causes death. Be careful what you let into your spirit through your ear gate.

Your mouth: Be careful what you speak out of your mouth. You are either speaking life or death. "…As he thinketh in his heart, so is he…", (Proverbs 23:7). And, "…Out of the abundance of the heart the mouth speaks", (Matthew 12:34).

Your emotions. This one is hard for many of us. They enemy know this and will try to push your buttons in this area. Proverbs 4:23 warns us "Above all else, guard your heart, for it is the wellspring of life". Ephesians 4:26-32 reminds us to not allow our emotions to control us.

Your sexual organs: We don't talk much about sex in church because it's an uncomfortable subject for some. But we should, because it is one of the greatest tools the enemy uses as a way to gain access to one's soul. Romans 12:1 admonishes us to present our bodies as a living sacrifice, holy and acceptable unto the Lord which is our reasonable service. We also see where 1 Corinthians 6:18 says: "Flee sexual immorality. Every sin that a man does is outside the body, but he who commits sexual immorality sins against his own body." It says to *flee* immorality. Flee means to get away from, as far as possible quickly.

The enemy understands that sex is pleasurable and it's the quickest way to form soul-ties. Soul-ties outside of marriage is dangerous and is the surest way to derail or destroy one's destiny. Ever notice in the demonic kingdom whenever there is wickedness in great measure it also coupled with orgies or some form of sexual perversion? That is no coincidence. If the enemy wants to destroy your purpose all he needs to do is send someone into your life to distract you sexually and its over. Many great, influential leaders have fallen because of the weakness of their flesh, especially because of sexual immorality or some form of infidelity. Paul said it best: "…But if they cannot control themselves, they should marry, for it's better to marry than to burn with passion," 1 Corinthians 7:9

Guarding these portals or entryways prevents demons from accessing and destroying one's destiny and eventually their lives.

COVENANTS
A covenant is an agreement or a legal binding document which gives someone the right to execute a particular action. There are good covenants and evil covenants. A good covenant would be covenants made that are influenced by heaven's agenda. Evil Covenants are agreements that have been set in place to give access-way to demonic curses or influences.

Demons understand that they cannot just access a realm without a portal and without a covenant. There are jurisdictional laws that prevent that from happening without a legal host who has authority to grant them access. So, they must legally come into agreement with a person to gain entry so that they can wreak havoc. They gain access via portals when a human comes into an agreement with them.

As mentioned previously, in the spirit realm there are spiritual laws that govern all activities in the spirit world. When God wanted to gain legal entry or access in the earth, He sent an angel to engage Mary into agreeing with His plan (Luke 1:28). Mary agreed: "Be it unto me according to thy word," (Luke 1:38). She entered into covenant with Holy Spirit. There was an agreement made with a natural earthly body giving Him access. With that agreement, He entered the earth realm via a natural earthly body. Isn't it amazing that God, Himself abides by His own spiritual laws? That's the integrity of the God we serve.

Without a covenant, it is illegal for any spirit to enter earth's affairs. When covenants are made, altars are established as a point of reference and serve as a place of memorial (See Gen 12:8; Joshua 8:30-35; Genesis 26:25). Altars mark the place where the agreement was formed, or the sacrifice was made. These covenants represent a promise of blessings that was to follow us and our generations to come. For example, today we are still being blessed because of the covenant God made with Abraham.

Well, just as the Lord made covenants with our ancestors, such as Abraham, to bring us into generational blessings that are still blessing us today, the enemy also has established covenants that caused years of generational curses. These agreements were made with our ancestors and passed down from one generation to the next, wreaking havoc as it went along. With each generation the curse gained momentum and became worse. It continues, until a deliverer shows up in that bloodline, who has the insight and the power to break the curse.

It's important to note that a covenant is sometimes made willfully but at other times it could've been made through ignorance. Many times, the unsuspecting victim does not even realize that they are coming into an agreement with the enemy to form a curse. For example, someone playing with tarot cards or consulting a palm reader has no idea the portals that they are opening and the long-term effects of those decisions.

The Bible says my people are destroyed for lack of knowledge. The enemy's greatest weapon is the spirit of deception to make you think that none of this is true. He wants us to remain passive and ignorant of his devices. If you believe the lies of the enemy, you are already defeated. Think about it, why would the demonic encounter in the text we read previously in Luke 4 and several others be recorded in scripture if it wasn't relevant.

As Christians we tend to choose what we want to believe and accept from scripture, but we don't get to pick apart the Truth of God's Word. As spiritual beings we cannot dismiss the fact that demons exist and are causing havoc around us. Many of us choose not to believe in witchcraft. Why? Because the subject is uncomfortable and the thought process is that if we don't believe in, it can't affect us. That is the biggest lie from the enemy. Just because one doesn't believe or chooses to dismiss it, doesn't make it of non-effect. In fact, the opposite is true, it will be even more effective. Being ignorant to Satan's devices is a disadvantage to the believer, (see 2 Corinthians 2:11)

While one chooses to remain ignorant, the devil is exercising his legal right in your bloodline, tearing up your family. But, could it be that *you* are the one chosen to break these generational curses and to rid them from your bloodline?

Have you noticed certain sicknesses or disorders that seem to be prevailing from generation to generation in your family? Is there a medical explanation that suffices as an explanation? What's causing the same situation to affect all the men or women in your family? Isn't it interesting, that there is no natural explanation for certain things that occur in our families? For example, why is it that in some families, marriages do not last or in other families, death occurs prematurely, around the same age? For other families, there are highly intelligent family members who master middle or high school, but something goes wrong on college level, or they may even graduate college with a degree but are unsuccessful attaining a meaningful career. They are intelligent individuals, but there is no sign of prosperity in their lives to reflect it. Or you may see a family where the women have trouble conceiving. These are all patterns or signs of generational curses.

Until someone steps in and identifies what is happening and decides to stand in the gap to break these covenants, the enemy will continue to wreak havoc. Tell yourself, I am that one. I am the one chosen to destroy every bloodline curse in my family. And believe you have the tools needed to break these cycles in your family. YOU must decide that with new information, you will no longer hide out in deception. With new information, you have what it takes to not just be empowered but to take action to bring about change. You're not just doing this for you, but the future generations are relying on you to stand in the gap in this moment. Think about what will happen to your children or your grandchildren if you don't step in now and break the curse. Decide that as of today demonic activities in my bloodline, my home and in me stops. It will not make it to the next generation.

ALTARS

"And the Lord appeared unto Abram, and said, unto thy seed will I give this land: and there builded he an altar unto the Lord, who appeared unto him." **Genesis 12:7 (KJV)**

"Isaac built an altar, called on the Lord's name, pitched his tent, and had his servants dig a well. Genesis 26:25 (KJV)

Everything that happens in your life, whether good or bad starts with an altar. An altar is a meeting space where one has an encounter with a spiritual being. Altars are used by satanic agents as well as by servants of the Lord. As you know the enemy copies what God does.

Whenever you see hexes and curses in your bloodline. There is an altar of sin and inequity against your bloodline. Someone opened a door or portal giving access. The only way to reverse it is to build an altar unto the Lord. An altar unto the Lord dismantles and reverses anything the enemy previously had in place and opens a portal for supernatural blessings and favor.

Altars are traditionally a place where in scripture one has an encounter with the Lord. It's a place where "Thy Kingdom come, Thy will be done in earth as it is in heaven", is manifested. According to scripture, altars were usually tangible and made from wood or stones. It was a place of sacrifice and prayer and a place where covenants were made.

Some folks will say that was the Old Testament, today our altar is our hearts. While that may be true, I believe there should still be a physical space in our homes and churches where we spend time with God. Now, I do understand that your heart is a meeting space. But considering that we make room and space to sleep, to eat, for date nights, for work, shouldn't we have a special place to encounter His presence on a regular basis? Now you can have multiple altars in different spaces, based on your schedule and where you spend most of your time. But carve out somewhere and some time that is dedicated to having an encounter with Him.

CHAPER 11:
A CALL TO RETURN TO THE ALTAR

When you begin to spend time on your altar, you will begin to develop a closer walk with him. Jeremiah 33:3 says, "Call unto me and I will answer thee and show thee great and mighty things, which thou knowest not." God wants to reveal somethings to us and about us but there will only be a reveal when we make our way to our altars. The altar is a place where we have a divine encounter.

Most will disagree that there should be a designated place for worship. While I agree that worship should take place anywhere, I also believe there should be a specific place dedicated to alone time of prayer. Having a space devoted to meeting God whenever you. want to, is extremely important. It helps to provide discipline for you to quiet everything down and make a decision that this is your set place to get to and to spend time with the Father. Whether that be a prayer room, a prayer closet, in your car or wherever, I suggest having a designated place reserved for intimacy with Him.

Altars were and still are significant. When we read old testimony scripture we see where altars were set up whenever there was an encounter with God. They were also built as memorials to remind the people where God had met them (add scriptures). It's a place where He manifested Himself and made covenants with them. It is important to understand that we serve a covenant keeping God, who is holy. Holy means that He is integral which means He keeps covenants with His people for many generations. Deuteronomy 7:9

says, "Know therefore that the Lord thy God, he is God, the faithful God, which keepeth covenant and mercy with them that love Him and keep his commandments toa thousand generations…". How exciting is that, to know that the covenants you make on the altar with the Lord isn't just for you but it lasts for many generations.

The Lord uses altars as a place of covenants to bring forth promises and breakthroughs in our lives. It is important to note that the enemy does not have creative abilities, so he mimics whatever he sees the Lord doing. Whenever the enemy wants to come against you, altars are erected as a sign of covenant. Devil worshipers have altars upon which they wreak havoc and worship the enemy.

Now, let's talk about how covenants on the altar work in the spiritual realm. Covenants are binding agreements made when a person comes into agreement with a spiritual being. We come into agreement via our words, actions, and via disobedience. The enemy will use these things against us to assign demonic activities to our lives.

If there is a covenant working against us in the enemy's camp, the only way to break it is to renounce or disavow that covenant and destroy that altar with the blood of Jesus. As long as that covenant sits on that altar, the enemy has legal rights to torment and oppress and bring destruction into your life.

But no matter what type of altar or the amount of demonic oppression that is working against you, there is a more powerful altar from where the blood of Jesus speaks. You see when we are born again, we come into covenant with Jesus and the sacrifice He made on Calvary. Calvary represents an altar where His blood was shed for us. As a result, we have access to the power available via His precious blood. His blood speaks louder than any accusation the enemy can bring against you on the altar. His blood is the remedy to cancel out every curse in your bloodline. When you apply His blood, it dismantles everything the enemy had working against us. His blood scatters and destroys all demonic activity.

Now it's important to understand that in order for an altar to be erected against you, the enemy uses bodies. These bodies are people who when the enemy comes looking, he sees himself in them. What do I mean by this? The enemy is not going to curse you or your bloodline with promiscuity if sexual perversion is not something he finds in you. But if he does find it in you, he will use it to gain access and use it against you. When the enemy comes looking, if he sees lust. Lust leads to perversion and the enemy knows that he can use it as a vehicle to transport sexual filthiness: rape, incest, fornication, adultery and so on. That's why it's important that when we recognize and identify those proclivities prevalent in our bloodline, working against us and immediately seek to eradicate them.

If the enemy cannot find himself in you, he is illegal to operate there. He will search and search, looking or an entryway or door to not just enter your life but to gain a footing in your bloodline. You see when we are drawn away by our own lustful desires, we only see what it does to us. But the enemy understands that our "little sins" impact us for generations to come. Selah.

There are some behaviors that have been passed down through our blood line from generations ago. Because a door was opened by our parents or grandparents or even further back. Because no one repented of that sin, that demonic spirit has legal right to continue in our family from generation to generation. If we do not identify the blood line curse and renounce it and tear down its altar, it will continue to wreak havoc in our lives continually until someone breaks it.

We must be so careful what we say and what we do. Our words bring us into agreement sometimes even without our awareness. We must be careful of what belief systems we hold on to. I'm talking about family rituals and customs that have been passed down. Some of those are laced with demonic covenants.

Our actions too can cause us to come into covenant with the enemy. Say for example, we show up in spaces with friends who practice certain non-Christlike behaviors. Our presence there is endorsing the behavior. We must learn to say no to certain places and to certain practices. For example, some folks allow their children to dress up for Halloween and go trick or treating, not realizing they are allowing themselves and their innocent children to come into covenant with certain spirits. Oh, it's innocent, we say. It's just candy. It's just for fun. While the candy may be innocent, the practice is not. And who are the folks giving candy to our children? During Halloween, everyone is not just pretending. It's one of the days of the year when real witches and warlocks are celebrating. You don't know who is giving your child candy that was offered up to idols and "preyed" over by entities and while your child is innocent, they are unknowingly being inducted into some form of agreement in the spirit realm. Folks, we need to open up our eyes. Satan is not playing with us. He's simply relying on us to stay ignorant.

I know this sounds extreme. I am glad it does. Because the enemy is extreme. The Bible says he comes to Kill, steal and destroy (scripture). That sounds extreme to me.

Pray this simple prayer: "Lord, open up my eyes that I may see!"

So here we will make some declarations in prayer to break some things in our bloodlines:

First, take a few minutes and just acknowledge the king as you enter his presence. Psalm 100:4 tells us how to enter the King's presence.

Next let's take a moment to repent of any sins we may have committed, knowingly and unknowingly. Also repent of any bloodline curses in your family, (Psalm 51:1-12). When I did this, I went all the way back as far as I could go, back to Adam and Eve. I wanted to take no chances by missing anyone.

Now, take a few minutes to pray regarding each of the bullet points below, renouncing any agreement that was made when you or any family member entered a covenant with same. These are only suggested prayer points; you can use this same format to pray against covenants for other situations that may be affecting your life to which it may apply. Also, feel free to add additional things that Holy Spirit brings to the surface in prayer:

- Anti-marital magnets
- Divorce agreements
- Spirit of lust, perversion, incest
- Spirit of disagreements and divisions
- Spirit of jealousy, envy, competition
- anti-covenant covenants
- Soul ties and ungodly relationships
- Lust, fornication, adultery
- Third party relationships, cheating
- Children born out of wedlock

If you are married, you have the right to stand in the gap for your spouse as well and pray the same prayer regarding their bloodline, which is now your bloodline because of marital inheritance.

Pray against EVIL PATTERNS, (every time, around a certain time the enemy shows up in cycles to wreak havoc). Declare that no weapon fashioned against me, my children, my spouse, my destiny, my territory, finances, ministry/business shall prosper.

Begin to use your words to break every covenant working against your bloodline, such as: delay, stagnation, divorce, lack, deception, etc. Add as many you can.

Declare that: "Curses break now in Jesus' name. Hexes break now in Jesus' name. I call to an end season of frustration, brokenness, shame, barrenness, (add more). Because I am redeemed by the blood of Jesus Christ; I exercise my authority and engage the blood of Jesus Christ against every transaction made by me or anyone in my family. I strip you of your legal right to my bloodline. My angels are on assignment now, dismantling every evil altar raised up against me and my bloodline. The blood of the eternal covenant speaks for me now in Jesus' name. I build a new altar unto the Lord and come into agreement with His will concerning my life, in Jesus name"

As you pray, your angels have already been assigned to work for you to bring to nought the works of the enemy. Right where you are, build a new altar and establish a new covenant with the Lord concerning your marriage/future marriage, or regarding your health or whatever it is you are standing in the gap for concerning you and your family.

Begin to make decrees and declarations on your new altar that has been built unto the Lord. Decree the opposite of what the enemy had on the demonic altar. For example, if there was sickness, declare health. If there was poverty, declare wealth. If there was barrenness, declare fruitfulness.

Pray: "I decree and declare that my family walks in divine health. We will live long successful lives. I decree that marriages in my family will last. I decree and declare that my children and all the children in my family will finish college, get married and have successful business and careers. I decree and declare that the blessing of the Lord overtakes my family for many generations to come..."
Keep declaring and decreeing what comes to mind.

As you've established a new covenant with the Lord, be sure to honor it. On the days when you fall short, simply repent and keep going.

Now, begin to thank the Lord for the manifestation of what you have prayed for this day. Now seal it with praise. Praise Him for the finished work sealed by the blood of the Lamb. As you do, stand still, and see the salvation of the Lord.

Your faith becomes the catalyst that activates God's promise, allowing you to see the tangible manifestation going forward in your bloodline.

CHAPTER 12:
DEALING WITH OPPRESSIVE SPIRITS

Now let's go back to the scenario found in Luke 4.

Remember, we said demons can oppress a person from the outside (for example whispering in their ears) but notice where these demons were present in this case. They were speaking from within the man using his voice and his body. The Bible did not say it snuck upon him and pushed him from behind. It spoke through him.

Also please notice where the man was, He was in the Holy Place…in the synagogue … in the presence of HOLINESS… Jesus Christ Himself. The demons were in the presence of Deity and did not leave until Jesus commanded them to. They were having a conversation with Jesus.

Notice that they knew who He was as they were able to identify HIM. They spoke out clearly as to who He was in verse 34: "…let us alone: what have we to do with thee, thou Jesus of Nazareth? Art thou come to destroy us? I know thee who thou art: the Holy One of God." With that Jesus told them to hush and commanded them to come out of the man. They recognized and obeyed Jesus because these were ancient, fallen spirits from another realm, occupying this man's body.

But notice that although they knew who Jesus was and understood the authority and power He had, yet still they did not willingly leave the man until He commanded them to.

One of the biggest demonic influences around a believer is the spirit of witchcraft. Witches are not flying around on brooms with pointy hats with a huge pimple on their faces. Many are hanging out in the church. Hiding amongst the believers. They are leading the Intercessory team, leading the choirs and some are even preaching over the pulpits. Some are hiding behind acts of benevolence. They are deeply arrogant, religious and condescending folks. People of God wake up! The enemy disguises himself as an angel of light but is nothing but a deceiver, pretending to be something he is not! Wake up!

Galatians 5:19-21 KJV

"Now the works of the flesh are manifest, which are these; Adultery, fornication, uncleanness, lasciviousness, Idolatry, witchcraft, hatred, variance, emulations, wrath, strife, seditions, heresies, envyings, murders, drunkenness, revellings, and such like: of the which I tell you before, as I have also told you in time past, that they which do such things shall not inherit the kingdom of God."

In this chapter, there are mentions of several types of behaviors, but I choose for the sake of this writing to highlight *witchcraft*. Here in this passage, Paul was not speaking to unbelievers. He was talking to believers who were Galatians. Today this same word applies to us Christians no matter where we are.

These were Christians he was warning about the practice of witchcraft. There are so many in church operating under this spirit thinking its ok to mix it with Christianity.

Witchcraft is a spirit which controls and manipulates. Whenever you see someone that is super controlling and manipulating, it is a sign that person might be a witch. Oh, but they are so nice. Witches pretend to be nice. The enemy disguises himself as an angel of light and that is what makes him effective. He is not going to show up with red horns and a pitchfork.

Witches appear sweet and subtle but that is how they get their hook deeply rooted in you. They are extremely dangerous and spiteful individuals, especially when they do not get their way. They will go to any extent to control and manipulate. But if you want to see their true colors, place them in a situation where they have no control or they are unable to manipulate and you will see their wrath on full display. They become incredibly angry under these circumstances

In 1st Peter 5:8 we read, "Be sober-minded; be watchful. Your adversary the devil prowls around like a roaring lion, seeking someone to devour." The enemy is always on a mission to wipe out the saints of God.

So then back to the question is it mental illness or is it a demon that is manipulating the individual? Are medical professionals wrong? No, they are not wrong. But it is important to note that we live in the natural world but everything in the natural is influenced by the spiritual world. Mental illness is real but it is a sign there is demonic influence behind it. The signs tell us that at some point, a covenant was initiated and a demon or demons gained legal rights to oppress that person's mind.

Psalm 9:9 says, "The Lord is a stronghold for the oppressed." Oppression comes from the enemy via demonic influence. Mental illness is a form of oppression by demons. So, while mental illness is the branch on a tree the root is that there is a strongman... a demon lurking in the background that is causing it. All forms of infirmities that exist are powered by demonic activities. If I did not believe that statement prior to my experience in Jamaica, when I encountered up close and in person interaction with demons, trust me when I say, I do now.

Two months into this journey, I visited a friend. She was sick and the doctors confirmed she was experiencing the late stages of cancer. I went with a few friends to pray for her and seeing her condition and knowing that I wouldn't be back in Jamaica for some time, I was feeling very sad that perhaps this might be my last time seeing her. I spent some time with her and as it was time to go, I asked those with me to pray with me for her.

Now this entire time, my friend who was laying down, unable to sit up because her body was so weak from the infirmity. We drew closer to her bedside and formed a circle around her and began to pray.

A few minutes into the prayer, I heard myself say "Lord before we go any further, I ask you to cover the team with your blood." I did not understand why my prayer had shifted from praying for my friend to praying for the ladies visiting with me. But to answer the question, immediately we felt our hands being tossed strongly and we realized instantly, that we were no longer holding hands with a weak individual. Instead, We were now face to face with a talking demon fully manifesting from inside her body. Let me tell you, I was not expecting this. But thank God for Jesus, we jumped into deliverance mode.

The demon spoke to me "Why did you come here to torment me? Leave me alone." I asked, "Who are you?" He said, "Legions!" I wanted to pass out then, as I could not believe this was happening.   Up until that moment, I had never had such an experience with a demon in person. I only read in the Bible where the demons spoke to Jesus asking the same question and then referring to themselves as legions. It seemed like a joke except it was so real and we knew we had work to do. Right away the ladies and I began to pray in tongues and ask the Lord for divine intervention. It was no easy task, but Holy Spirit gave us wisdom and boldness as we began to pray and cast out those foul evil spirits. We had no idea how intense the process would be but by the grace of God we prevailed.

CHAPTER 13:
BACK TO THE DREAM

Now, let's go back to the dream I had. Please understand the dynamics of what was happening during this time in my life. I was under immense attack in my marriage and in my home.

As I said previously during this time, I knew of witches, (or so I thought), but my understanding was limited or dismissive. I thought if I didn't pour too much energy into thinking about the occult world it couldn't affect me. That was poor thinking/judgment on my part. I was in for a rude awakening. Very soon I was about to discover just how real witches and witchcraft is and how prevalent it could be amongst friends/family and folks that show up speaking in tongues in church! All I can say is this discovery was nothing short of a nightmare.

So, if you remember I mentioned that two different individuals, (my cousin and the other person from the prayer line), who were in two different parts of the world prophesied to me on the same day about what was happening around me. One called in the morning, and I received word about the second encounter that same afternoon. These individuals did not know each other but on the same day they shared the same word, concerning my situation. A word that only Holy Spirit could have revealed because neither one had any way of knowing what was taking place around me in the moment.

Both identified and mentioned that I was experiencing unusual warfare, the attacks were INTENTIONAL, and the willing bodies being used of the enemy were folks that were closely connected to both me and my husband. So, I began to seek the Lord about what was happening, who was behind it and what to do next.

As I sought the Lord, the revelations kept coming. To my surprise and dismay as to who some of the willing vessels were. You would be surprised to find out who is jealous of you and who secretly envy's you. I am not talking about the obvious "haters". I mean the folks you trust, who walks closely with you, who desires to have what you have and to be elevated with you, without the process. They talk about you while you are going through and watch you go through the hell, but then when God promotes you after the testing, they want to fall in line with you on the same level as you. This discovery was very sobering and taught me that at this season of my life, I had to mature quickly and not be so naïve to the enemy's devices. I found myself in a crash course learning things I thought I was sheltered from.

As I stated previously, I was never one who highlighted witchcraft or witches as a source behind my problems. But after what I've experience in this last season of my life, my eyes are fully opened, and I see things so differently now. Some days I wish I could close my eyes and unsee what I can now see. Sometimes I can spot a demon on a person as I am shopping in the supermarket. It's as if my spiritual senses have been awakened to demonic activity. My discernment has been heightened to recognize which spirit is in operation in the moment. I can now recognize when a person is speaking, versus when a demon is speaking through a person.

I truly did not understand what was happening around

me. I knew it was intense and unusual but did not understand the depth or magnitude of it all. I was in a test while at the same time dropped into the school of Holy Spirit to learn firsthand lessons on spiritual warfare and demonology. I was not prepared for the journey. However, if you are reading this it simply means the blood prevailed! It also means that there is a reason your hands picked up this particular book. Your now and your destiny is connected to the information in this book.

Did I like the experience? Of course not! But I thank God for it. The Bible says in all things give thanks. I am better now for it too. I am more alert. I am wiser and better equipped to manage spiritual matters in this new dimension I'm in. Truth be told, the higher up you go you will experience new devils. For each dimension, the demon will be more intense than the previous. But the good news is that Jesus defeated them all and by His grace so can you.

CHAPTER 14

THE UNFOLDING OF THE DREAM

Remember the part in my dream where I mentioned someone died and they were in the large room inside a red coffin? It was later revealed to me who the individual was. Not long after, I received a prophetic word that the witch sent a spirit against me, for my demise. Another person prophesied on two other occasions that I escaped death. Do you know how I escaped? I escaped because of the prayers of the righteous. Though the weapon was formed against me it could not prosper.

The fury in me, to think that the witch or witches thought they could take me out. I have news for them, I have kingdom work to do. That is one of the blessings of your altar is that it gives your divine immunity to the enemy's devices. The enemy cannot kill who God has anointed to live. I have purpose yet to be fulfilled. My assignments includes this book written to expose the kingdom of darkness. I could not die before my time. Instead, on my altar, I prayed that everything sent against me be returned to its sender!

Now, if you remember, I dreamt about the filthy apartment. That lined up with what was prophesied that the witch brought something into my home. Though my home in the natural was not dirty, the environment was filthy because the witch tarnished it with whatever was brought into my space.

I also dreamt of snakes and as we explored earlier, we discovered that snakes represented witchcraft. The good news is that in the dream I killed every single one, which meant that I would prevail over everything that was sent against me. A year later, I am still standing. Glory to God!

Remember also, my husband was experiencing some form of trance while lying on the bed. Then later in the dream he disappeared. I said to someone in my dream, when they asked where he was: "He left me here to fight all these snakes." Well throughout this entire time I had to fight on this end alone. He left home and while he was away, I had to fight for my mind, my home, my marriage, the ministry and continued to pray him through.

As I said before, I am not making excuses or finding a way to justify what happened in my relationship. I left everything in God's hands. However, to see the unfolding is just remarkable to me as I felt the Lord prepared me for what was to come. Did it make it easier to go through? I'm not sure if I can say so, but at least it gave me some kind of grounding as I navigated this very difficult season of testing.

I will also say that the breakdown of my marriage was not solely due to these witches behind the scenes. Some of it was due to our own negligence, insecurities and shortcomings inspired by or giving way to demonic influence and interference.

There was a part of the dream where I said I must go to church, and I was searching for a black skirt to cover up to get to church. The revelation of the see-through white dress came. First, it represented the fact that I was going to go through a very vulnerable season, leaving me exposed. I was not going to be able to cover up the shame and embarrassment this time. God was going to allow others to see what I was going through. He wanted this to be public.

It's one thing to go through behind close doors. But to go through publicly is something else.

But all along, God had a plan of restoration, but if it's private He would not get any glory from it. He wanted the world to see it all break down publicly and then watch as He restores it, publicly. Why though would God allow this and why so public? He did it because of all the marriages that will be restored when they see how GOD brought ours back from the ashes.

He said it like this earlier that year: "From The Ashes…EMERGE!" The scripture to back this up was 1 Peter 5:10, "After you have suffered a little while, the God of all grace, who has called you to His eternal glory in Christ, will Himself restore, confirm, strengthen and establish you". That was the theme and scripture He gave me earlier in the year for the conference. But it was more than a conference them, He was making a declaration!

Ashes are the end results of a really bad fire. Whenever any substance is burnt to ashes, its at its worst state. It becomes irreparable. It is unrecognizable, as it no longer looks anything like what it once was or what it should be. At that point, you just walk away and start over because there is nothing to work with. But the God who is Sovereign can work with Ashes. Can he not? I remember He fashioned man out of dirt. So, can He not fashion something great out of ashes? I am super excited to experience the end result of what God is getting ready to do! Let's go to church for two seconds with a praise break. In my preacher voice, tell your neighbor, the witches influenced by the legions of demons DID NOT win! Now shout with me on that.

In the meantime, I must say, one couldn't imagine the pain, the hurt and the shame I felt when I still had to go forward and show up for my ministry assignments. Let me pause here and share a little about that. In the middle of this warfare, I received numerous assignments to preach at other churches/conferences. The Lord also birthed out a church through me. A new church was not something I saw coming. Trust me, it was the last thing on my mind. Many onlookers had their "TEA" about this decision, but all I can say is, it was simply the working of the Lord.

Prior to the separation, we had been pastoring a small church with a small group of members. During the breakup, the folks stopped attending the church. During that time, the Lord spoke to me about gathering those folks and continuing to shepherd them because while we were busy warring, we were still responsible for those souls. So, I would connect with and minister to them on zoom on Sundays at the same time as the usual church with the intention that when the Lord restored the marriage, we would all just fall back in line. God had other plans.

In the middle of the warfare, I was praying for my marriage. I wanted God to fix it as He had done before and bring us back together. One morning, I received a phone call from a friend. She said, "Check your email." She said she had been praying for me and the Lord told her to send over paperwork on how to start a church. I had not told her that the Lord was speaking to me about launching a church. I laughed and said to her that I did not have a church name. She said, "That's ok, fill out the form and when He gives you the name of the church you add it."

I didn't want to obey those instructions as I thought they were a sign that my marriage was over. I knew that a new church, with a new name would mean there was no room for reconciliation as it would only create more problems. I did not want my marriage to be over. So, I ignored what she said. Two days later a young lady, good friend of mine reached out to me and said, "I just sent you $100 electronically". I thanked her and asked for what. She said the Lord told her in prayer to sow into the building fund. Now mind you, I had no building or knew where to find a building, but I knew these messages were confirming what God was already speaking to me.

You see, weeks prior, I was praying and heard the Lord instruct me to get my journal and begin to write. He began to speak to me about a church that He would give me that would be remarkably similar to a hospital. He said people would come in one way but would leave there changed. He said it would be a hospital with specific areas addressing specific needs. He began to download the instructions on how to set it up. I had not shared with the folks what the Lord was saying so I know the Lord was using them to confirm what He shared with me. Still, I ignored each person, in disobedience, because I wanted what I wanted God to do: fix my marriage and restore me back to my husband's church.

Two days later another friend gave me an envelope in person with $200 for the building fund. All these occurrences occurred days apart and the individuals were not aware that they were each being used to confirm what the Lord said to me in prayer, prior. Still, I thought ok maybe the Lord is giving my husband and I a new building for the current ministry that was previously established. We did receive word three times that year that the building was coming.

The next day, as I awoke from my sleep, a name dropped into my spirit. I heard: "Outreach Prophetic Deliverance Ministries and its Global." I went to google it and realized that business name did not exist. It was in that moment I broke down crying. Everything in me felt like defeat. God why would you give me a name separate from the current name. I already know my husband is not going to come and merge under the new name. I was heartbroken and disappointed. I thought this is probably how Abraham must have felt when the Lord told him to sacrifice his promise (son). I truly felt like I had an unfair choice to make: marriage or ministry. I did not want to choose, I wanted both.

The Lord then literally dropped in my spirit to reach out to the apostles of the church where I am now, to ask for space. Even that was a setup. I had no idea God would use them to favor me, and to welcome me into their space. I am truly grateful for the kindness they have shown since we've been there. God worked it all out and the church is steadily growing. Praise God!

I shared that story to say when God has a plan, He puts everything in place and grants you favor. As a result, "Global Outreach Prophetic Deliverance Ministries" was born. Not just a church space but it's the beginning of a deliverance movement!

Every single detail in my dream transpired in some form or other. The chocolate brown gift containing snakes, the missing sheet (that showed up two months later), the five snake heads panting for air, every single detail of the dream unfolded. Even the warning that I gave my friend about the snake that was sneaking up on her near the sand. Even the very words I used from the dream, warning her, played out in another conversation. It was after the conversation ended; I realized those were the words of warning from the dream with the same desperate plea.

The only thing that's yet to manifest is the scene with the red coffin. Truth is, I do not wish anything bad on anyone, but I do know that judgment comes to those who oppose God's will. He said, "Whom I've joined together, let no man put asunder," (Matthew 19:6). It's one thing when the responsible parties decide to end the marriage. It's another thing when a witch decides to interfere for their own selfish reasons. His word also says, "Thou shalt not suffer a witch to live," (Exodus 22:18). Some things are out of our hands, they are simply the price one pays for interfering with and opposing God's will. Now folks can repent and hopefully, God will forgive and reverse the decree.

As you can summarize by now, this season I had been dealing with not just one witch but with multiple witches. This is a crazy thought as the "witches" were all "church goers." I can only share my story and hope you or anyone you know never have to go through anything similar. This attack was one that I would never want anyone else to experience. But the sad truth is, unfortunately, someone else is going through or will go through something similar. Since demonic activities cannot be totally avoided, then my hope is that this book will be a tool to help you navigate what's happening and it will help you re-discover your altar as you go through it. The key words are "go through it." I don't care how difficult it becomes during the process, keep going. Do not drop your assignments. Do not drop your praise. Keep going!

During the attack, I had to keep going. Do you remember when Covid hit, and folks were dying? One of the instructions given was if you get sick, do not stay in bed. Get up and keep moving so your organs can keep fighting and continue to function. Well, that is how I felt during this time. My assignments kept coming and I could not afford to sit still. Why not? Because I know that's what the enemy wanted: to shut me down and make me give up in the process. That wasn't going to happen. Also, I understood that my pain was meant to produce purpose in others, the ones assigned to my voice.

This fight was not just about my marriage. The enemy has enough married couples in his camp. This fight was because the enemy recognized that the ministry was and still is making an impact and he wanted to shut it down. He thought if he broke up the marriage, it would destroy the ministry. He was in for a rude awakening, and all his imps who were assigned to launch this attack, reported back to headquarters discombobulated and dismembered. I was prepared to fight all the way through with determination and certainly on my worse day I did exactly that. With a broken heart I kept on fighting. With tears, I kept on fighting. Feeling misunderstood and rejected but I kept on fighting. I fought until the flames on my altar grew into a blaze. In the end, the enemy earned a black eye. And I'm sitting back in amazement of the awesome God that I serve.

When attacks come into your life, whatever you do, don't quit. Keep going. Storms will always come but use them as a catalyst to get you to where you need to go. One thing is for sure, you are not alone in the storm. You have a Paracletus, the One who stands alongside you who will be with you throughout the process. If you can endure to the end, you will enter your season of promotion and you will reap a great reward. I am exiting this season with a new book and as a new radio station host, another assignment that dropped into my lap unexpectedly. Jeremiah 29:11, (MSG) says it best, "I know what I am doing. I have it all planned out. Plans to take care of you, not abandon you, plans to give you the future you hope for." Don't tell me what God won't do, if you can endure to the end. Are you willing to go through the process?

As I said before, if we want to see revivals break out all over this nation, if we want to see souls saved and delivered for real, if we want to see miracles signs and wonders then we need to set the altar ablaze. Set it on fire with our prayers.

CHAPTER 15:
WHEN CHRIST ALLOWS US TO EXPERIENCE HIS HEART FOR HIS BRIDE

Sometimes Christ allows us to feel the weight of the assignment that He's placed on our lives. This means at times we may have to walk through very difficult situations and sometimes feel isolated or rejected until we get to the finish line.

No matter how we feel, or how much it hurt, we must press through to the other side. We can't give up during the storm. Too much is at stake. Too many are depending on us. We must understand that ministry is not a "gig" or an opportunity to "make something of yourself". It's a decision that has an eternal affect on one's soul. We can't gamble with that. I often tell the women I minister to that sometimes my heart breaks just so yours can heal. Think about that. Ministry is sacrifice. Consider just how much Jesus gave up for you and me.

When we begin to feel the weight of the assignment we will then begin to take it seriously. At that time our prayers must align with the thought: "Not my will, but Thy will be done." This was Jesus' response when He had a moment in Gethsemane. He was starting to feel the pressure of His assignment and asked for a way out. We have all been there where we wanted the season to end prematurely because of the pressure we feel in the moment. But as believers we must take that same posture as Jesus took, with the understanding that at all times, we always submit to God's Sovereign will. This can be a hard prayer especially when we desire a particular outcome. Sometimes things will turn out the way we want. Other times it will not. But at all times, when we submit to the process, the outcome should always bring God glory, and it will be for our good.

An example of this is, eight months after the separation from my spouse, one morning he texted me to say he wanted a divorce. Whether he was saying it just to say it or whether he really wanted it, it made me frustrated because this was not the first time he had said it. So, I reluctantly said: "Sure let's get it done."

The morning, we agreed to meet at the courthouse, as I started to get dressed this deep feeling came over me as if I were heading to the funeral of a loved one I cared about deeply. It reminded me of the day I was getting ready to go to my great-grandma's funeral. It was the worst feeling in the world. That day after completing the initial paperwork to initiate the process, returning home I realized the date. It was June 6th. It was the third-year anniversary of when we started pastoring our first church together. That made me even more sad. I wept all the way home.

At the court, they gave us a 40-day period before the final decision was made. So, on that day it was our 3-year church anniversary and 40 days to final decision. As I went to curl up in my bed, I heard the Lord say: "You can die here in the wilderness, or you can exit and enter the Promised Land". I did not fully understand what He meant.

Over the next few days, I started to come around as that scripture began to play in my mind: "What therefore God hath joined together, let not man put asunder", (Matthew 19:6). I started to feel guilty and realized that even I didn't have the right to put asunder what God had joined together.

We took vows on the altar. We came into covenant with God before our friends, family and Pastors. We were breaking a divine covenant that we had made. There was an altar working against us. The altar of divorce was trying to make its way in. It was up to us at this point to reverse it or succumb to it. I chose to fight on the altar. To date, a year later, four months after we initiated the process we have not gone back to complete the additional paperwork. I decided I would pray until God reveals the end results.

I had to repent and go back to my Source and decide to raise up another altar instead. I heard the Lord say, "Meet me in prayer for the next 21 days". Right away, I assumed He meant a 21-day fast. But the Lord said, "No, meet me every night between 12 midnight and 3:00 AM". I said, "Ok Lord." Every night it didn't matter what time I fell asleep; I would wake up during that time to pray.

The first several nights I was in intense warfare prayer, warring against the demonic altars that were contending for my mind, ministry and my marriage. This continued for at least a week and a half. After several days, I heard the Lord say, tonight when you come into prayer, no more warfare prayers. Tonight, I want you to come in and just worship.

That night, as I laid across my bed, I started to worship but my body was tired. I felt drained. I heard the Lord instructing me to put some worship music on. I obeyed, and as I did each song that came on began to minister to me. They each were songs that reminded me that He was a good Father and how merciful He was towards me. They were love songs that He sang over me. (Zephaniah 3:17).

As I listened to the songs, I fell asleep and that night I rested all night long like a baby. The next morning, I woke up saying, "Lord I was supposed to be worshiping but I fell asleep." With a gentle nudge He said "Ah my child. You've been in intense warfare, and you were depleted. I needed to replenish you. So last night I had angels ministering to you".

I was so overwhelmed by the love and grace of God. He would take the time to pour back into me to replenish me. We do not understand how intense the spirit world is. When warring in the spirit it pulls from your natural man. For days prior, I was walking around feeling drained and super exhausted. I had never experienced anything like what I went through so I wasn't prepared, nor did I understand the dynamics of what it took to get through what I was facing.

During this time of separation, the Lord had me to understand how He feels when someone backslides, pulling away from the love affair they once shared with Him. I now understand the longing for reconciliation. I now understand how He feels to be separated from His bride yearning for her to come home. The longing, the hurt was unreal. The initial stage of the divorce process had me to experience the feeling of death that comes from separation.

This is the death that happens when we are separated from God. We could be walking around functioning but dying on the inside. That is what the enemy wants. He understands separation very well and wants to cause us to go through that same pain and agony. He understands he can never get back to what he lost and so will try to stop us from being reconciled to the Father and to our loved ones.

In this process, I understood the scripture also that says: "Turn, O backsliding children, saith the LORD; for I am married unto you", Jeremiah 3:14a. Though my spouse and I were at this point in our marriage journey I wanted things to turn around. I wanted reconciliation. My natural man would say it would be better to exit because there had been so much damage. It was better to replace than to repair. But my spirit man kept saying there will be glory after this. I kept thinking how we sometimes go astray and how God still doesn't give up on us. The word says He's married to us. He still sees us as His bride even when we are not upholding the covenants we've made with Him. But yet still, not one time does He turn His back on us.

The Lord shared a scenario with me that marriages of old didn't last because they were perfect.   They lasted because they decided to make it work. In today's society, folks no longer bother to fix what's broken. We are instead quick to replace it. If our smart phones have a crack, instead of repairing it, we trade it in for a new one. We quickly forget how much (financial) investment went into the now cracked phone. We would rather take a risk and pay the price for a new one instead of taking the time to repair it and re-use it. So, we are in relationships. Marriages are no longer lasting, because we give up too soon. One flaw and its over. Suddenly, the grass looks greener on the other side. By the time we realize it was nothing but paint, it's too late. By then then other party has moved on to the new.

But if we can take the broken pieces to the Designer who orchestrated the institution of marriage and trust Him to do the repairs, we would have something that the world could only dream of. It may show signs of wear and tear but that's the scar that proves we have a testimony. Don't discount the value your testimony adds to it. The scars would only serve as a reminder to give glory to God.

One cannot survive this Christian Walk without prayer, let alone survive a marriage without prayer. I now say that, but didn't understand the truth behind that statement until things were far out of hand. I waited until it was too late. I heard the warnings but did not take them seriously. I've heard people say it but, in the moment, I was so focused on being a good wife and ministry partner that I didn't prioritize constantly submerging my marriage in prayer the way I should have. Yes, I prayed for my husband. I prayed for his health and strength and daily bread. But didn't understand that I needed to war against witches and warlocks or general spiritual attacks concerning him.

Nadine, why are you sharing all of this? I am sharing with the hopes that the information will help to restore one marriage. If someone benefits and a marriage is resuscitated as a result, then it's a win. I pray someone reading this who is at the end of the rope with their marriage decide to take another look at it. My hope is that healing will take place and restoration will take place. Remember, He is a God of reconciliation. Yes, I know it takes two but let allow the process to start with you. Dust off the altar and do your part and let God do His part as He works on the other party. You have the power to change your situation and dismantle the plans of the demonic world.

Oh, what a rude awakening when one realizes just how real the demonic world is. And an even ruder awakening when you realize that the folks' demons use are the people in church worshiping right next to you.

Now, I'm not here to tear up the Body because indeed there is a remnant that has not bowed to baal and belzebubs. Not everyone in church is a witch or devil worshiper, but there are some present that have been sent to destroy the house and the men and women serving in the house. Folks who seek "power" and position will go after it at the expense of innocent souls.

As I reflect on all that's happened, I think of the year 2020, the year we got married. That was a year that great fear was upon the earth. There was a global pandemic. Not knowing who was going to live or die caused fear to circle the globe. Fear is the vehicle that transport demonic activity. Its's the opposite of faith that allows God to move. Fear caused many to lose their lives. Not only that, but during these fearful times a lot was revealed. The pandemic opened us up to a lot of things that were hidden in the natural, but also because of fear opened portals in the spirit realm giving access to all forms of seducing spirits and doctrines of devils: I Timothy 4:1 is where we find the words, "seducing spirits." It says, "Now the Spirit speaketh expressly that in the latter times, some shall depart from the faith, giving heed to seducing spirits and doctrines of devils."

We can all agree that the signs are everywhere that we are in the last days. Only those who have eyes to see and ears to hear what the Spirit of the Lord is saying will be able to stand during these evil and perilous days. As the scripture says many will depart from the Faith. The sad thing is they won't just quit and walk away. Some will still hide out in religion pretending to still be followers of Christ. They will look like and sound like Christians, but their hearts are no longer with Christ.

They will be in religious places and positions leading the flock and unbeknownst to them they are being controlled by demons. You will not be able to identify them in the natural world because their whoops and hollers will sound the same. They will be even bigger tithers and givers of offering. They will lead the prayer group. We are living in a sad day. If you don't have discernment, you will miss the witches and the warlocks actively serving in the house of the Lord. When they are revealed many of us will be in denial that they are who they are.

It's time to wake up as a Body. We have become too carnal, and folks are only interested in doing what makes them feel good. We are in a time of social acceptance and inclusion, so much that we are afraid to call out sin even when it has been identified. The enemy is not playing fair and has no respect of people so why are we being so passive and complacent? We cannot allow ourselves to become compromising and Lukewarm Christians, so we can fit in with the world. We were never meant to fit in. Christians have always been persecuted because we always oppose the wiles of the enemy.

I don't know why, especially in these dark days, as believers we have this expectation that our walk is going to be cushioned and comfortable. Picture this: "Christians who practice self-care 24/7". The enemy loves those kinds of Christians. He doesn't even bother them because he already knows they're so self-absorbed they're not a bother to him. He's concerned about the believer whose eyes and ears are open to the things of God, who are willing to take a stand against his dark kingdom.

2 Timothy 4:3 says:
"For the time will come when they will not endure sound doctrine; but after their own lusts shall they heap to themselves teachers, having itching ears; And they shall turn away their ears from the truth, and shall be turned unto fables."

We want things to be our way so bad that we compromise on all levels. We compromise the way we dress. There is nothing wrong with being stylish and cute, but we want to fit in with the world. Super short shorts, super tight clothing, and super exposed cleavage. Now some may say "nothing is wrong with that" but that is a clear indication that that person has a virus in their system.

Another indication there is a virus is that there will be compromise in their speech. They are afraid to speak out about sin. Their sermons no longer align with the gospel. They will instead constantly preach about houses, cars and land and about our haters. We could preach a whole sermon and never mention the name of Jesus. Something is wrong with that. Preaching should always be about Him. It should always point someone to the cross.

We compromise our relationships and so much more. We no longer stand for righteousness. We simply just want to be a part of the in crowd.

But God is challenging us to step up. Understanding the power of your altar is critical in this hour. Those who are most powerful, who God is going to use in this last hour are those who operate from the altar.

So, as far as my marriage was concerned, as hard as it was, I kept on praying. I believed that no matter what demonic altars were raised against the marriage, there was an altar that was far greater. And that altar sprinkled with the blood of Jesus was speaking loudly on my behalf. I decided that I would war on that altar for the covenant I made with my spouse and with God. I would do my part and like Shadrach, Meshach, and Abednego whatever the outcome, I trusted God's Sovereign will.

God is sovereign. God may or may not change the outcome. But one thing is for sure, if we submit to His process, He will change us and our perspective on the situation. If nothing else, the situation will draw us back to the altar. Please understand we will not always get what we want but as long as His will is in place, we understand that His Sovereignty is at work.

Back when I prayed for my dear friend in Jamaica, we believed God for her healing and trusted that would be the end result. Months later, she passed away. I was so broken and disappointed by her passing. I couldn't understand why God would take her home. I then had to acknowledge that God is sovereign. The outcome was not what was expected.

I prayed and God answered. Not what I expected but I accept His will. I gave my best but sometimes your best seems good until we experience God's best. We see the trees in front of us but God sees the entire forest. Sometimes winning is letting go of what is hindering you from entering God's best. Doesn't mean what was, didn't serve its purpose. It did. But sometimes new seasons usher in the new. Just because it wasn't good for you doesn't mean it's not perfect for someone else.

Praying God's will be done, will sometimes break us, our will, our desires. It will hurt at times. I can't begin to tell you how painful this season has been between losing my friend and seeing what became of my marriage. Even now, still praying for God to intervene and not knowing how He will. It can be hard to release what we hope for but at some it sometimes is necessary in order to embrace the new.

Releasing the old can be hard, but if we could only take a glimpse of what God has waiting for us. He is Sovereign in all He does and the word says, "No good thing will he withhold from those who walk uprightly."

Today I take the time to pray for someone who is going through a difficult situation and not knowing how to let go and move forward. It may be a bad relationship. It may be trauma that has held you captive from childhood or for many years. It may be from losing a loved one or from being harmed by a loved one, who may have passed away without resolving the damage they caused.

I know it hurt and know it's hard but trust the One who can heal your heart. He wants to heal you, but you must release the hurt. Make the trade today. Say this simple prayer with me:

"Father today I come to you broken, hurting (tell him what's causing you to hurt). I realize it's time for me to trade my pain for your joy. Lord I forgive (name the person(s) and most importantly I forgive myself from all the shame and all the blame. Lord today go into my most innermost part and heal me from the inside out. In Jesus name, amen".

With that simple prayer God is doing a quick work in a short time. Remember healing is the children's bread. The Lord is saying to you today: "Receive your healing THIS DAY, my child". Now allow his love to permeate you in those areas of your heart like never before.

As we close out this chapter, remember, when God doesn't change the circumstances, He will change you in it, and eventually your perspective on the situation will line up. We may not always understand God's will, but we must trust that He knows what's best for us. When the process seems blurred, simply trust the Processor.

CHAPTER 16:
RE-LOCATING YOUR ALTAR

As a child, I remember going to church and when there were prayer meetings, we were called down to a designated space known as the altar where we had to kneel and pray. We would spend hours in our knees kneeling before the Lord and crying out to Him.

Today the altar is not even acknowledged or identifiable in the house of worship. We have designated areas for praise n worship. We have the area where the musicians sit. We have the lavish pulpit area where our elaborate sermons are rendered. But there is no visible place for an altar where prayer is offered up in the sanctuary.

And yes, I know we are living under the dispensation of grace where our heart is the altar. The Bible tells us in Romans 12:1 to present our bodies a living sacrifice Holy and acceptable unto the Lord. I understand all of that and I am in favor of that. However, when the Bible tells us in Jeremiah 17:9, "The heart is deceitful above all things, and desperately wicked: who can know it?"

We know many of our hearts have waxed cold and have turned away from God. Many are following after seducing spirits, promising us houses, land and fame. These spirits tries to convince us that it doesn't take all of that anymore. The altar is no longer necessary. There is no need to spend hours in prayer. Prayer time is limited to 10-15 mins while the rest of the program lasts for hours.

I beg to differ. In these last days, we need a deeper level of consecration in prayer. Satan understands he's at the end of his rope and it's now or never. He has launched demons that we haven't experienced before and they are on a mission to recruit as many folks to the dark side before time wraps up. Now is the time to pray double-time for our loved ones to be saved and delivered. Now is the time to raise up an altar unto the Lord for our families, ministries and communities.

Do you know that there are people serving in churches who have skipped the altar before serving? They are serving but have not prayed in days, weeks? These folks live a filthy lifestyle all week long but know how to dress it up on Sunday mornings in lavish attire for service. They have broken covenant with God. They have raised up other altars before him. Altars that promotes money, power and fame. They worship their possessions; they worship statuses and other images.

We are in a day and time when many are questioning their faith. I am giving and serving but not seeing results. We are in expectations of the glorious manifestation, wanting to see miracles, signs and wonders but nothing.

God is saying today re-build me an altar! If you rebuild my altar, then I can restore the covenants that I made with your parents and grandparents and even the ones I made with you. Pay your vows and you will begin to see the blessings I promised you begin to manifest. If you want to see God move… Re-build the broken Altar!!!

In 1 Kings 18:30-40, we see a showdown of the altar. We see where Ahab was a wicked king who married a wicked woman name Jezebel. She introduced baal worship to the people of Israel. The Israelites forgot what the Lord said in Exodus 20:3 KJV, "Thou shalt have no other gods before me".

Jezebel erected strange altars to the worship of baal. She got rid of all the true prophets of God. Israel was now filled strange altars allowing idol Worship. God was not pleased. So here comes Elijah, the prophet of God, who shows up on the scene to challenge the altars of their false god.

Elijah sent for the people of Israel and tell them I want you to come close, we're about to have a showdown this day. Since you've forgotten the God of your forefathers and turned to worshiping idols, let's see which GOD is real. Which is able to answer by fire.

So, they sent for the 450 prophets of baal and told them to dress a bullock and place it on the wood. Do not add any fire to it. Elijah would also dress a bullock and lay it on the altar with no fire added to the wood. He said, "Now the God that answers by fire let Him be GOD." The people agreed.

The false prophets called on their god from morning till noon to consume the bullock, but nothing happened. Elijah began to mock them telling them to cry louder because perhaps bail maybe sleeping. They continued to cry out to their god, cutting themselves until evening and still nothing happened. They even jumped up and down on the altar, nothing happened.

Elijah then called the people and instructed them to come close. He drew them close. He was saying now it's my turn to call on my God, the one true and living God. He wanted them to witness God's power. He then repaired the altar of the Lord that was broken down.

He then built a trench (a gutter for water to flow) around the altar. He laid the pieces of bullock (sacrifices) on the altar and then he told them to fill up barrels with water and pour it on to the sacrifice on the altar. He wet up the wood and the offering. He then told them to repeat the process, pour more water onto it a 2nd and a third time. He wanted everything to be completely drenched in water. He wanted it to be soaked.

Now keep in mind that He was expecting God to answer by fire. Water repels fire. It's hard for fire to burn if the materials are soaked. He then filled up the trench with water.

The next thing Elijah did was pray. As he prayed, the fire of the Lord fell and consumed the offering and licked up every drop of water in the trenches. What was soaked was now completely dried. When the people saw it, they fell on their faces and acknowledged that there is only one true God.

Some of us have lost our fire on the altar. We have become distracted by what's happening around us. We have replaced the altar of the Lord with idol worship, witchcraft and forms of entertainment.

The Lord is saying to His Body today especially to you reading this, "Raise me an altar. Come back to the altar. My altars are full of ashes. Where is the flame? The flames have gone out. Until you rebuild the altar and get rid of the ashes, the enemy will continue to wreak havoc in your home, marriage, ministry, business and community. Build me an altar, a place of prayer and divine exchange".

Even the demonic world understands the power of the altar. Whenever the enemy wants to bring something upon you there is an altar that is erected against you. Witches and warlocks build shrines in their homes, but the believer has no altar.

It's time to return back to the altar. The altar is a holy place set up for the worship of God. It's a place of divine exchange. It's where covenants are made. It's where final decisions concerning your situation and God's will for your life is made.

CHAPTER 17:
HOW DO WE RE-BUILD THE ALTAR

Now, I don't know what caused your fire to go out and what has caused your altar to break down. But it can be repaired.

"And they shall take away the ashes from the altar, and spread a purple cloth thereon: "Numbers 4:13 (KJV)

It's time to remove the ashes and repay the vows you have made before the altar broke. The ashes represent our sins where we have strayed away from God.

Bitterness can tear down your altar. Unforgiveness can tear down your altar. The spirit of offense can destroy or altar. Undealt with Trauma can leave so many ashes on your altar making it impossible to light a flame. Dabbling with the occult is another way one can tear down or replace their altar. Sexual perversion is another way the enemy comes in to get a foothold to destroy your altar. These situations can cause the infrastructure of your altar to weaken and eventually break it down.

God wants us to repair our altars. It starts with repairing our relationship with Him. He wants to repair in us everything that's broken. He wants to repair our broken hearts so we can receive His word.

The first step to rebuilding the altar is to acknowledge that we became distracted and went astray for the ordinances of God. The next thing to do is repent. To repent means to turn away from what we are doing and go in the opposite direction. It means to abandon our way of doing things and now turn to the Lord's way of doing things. It's time to repent for not carrying out our end of the bargain. He still wants to bless us. He still wants to make us fruitful but He's waiting for us to turn back to Him.

It's a simple prayer asking the Lord: "Rebuild this broken vessel, Lord. So that I can be filled with your glory. Rebuild the altar of my heart so I can offer up sacrifices of praise."

Find a space that is dedicated to you worshiping Him on a consistent basis. After repentance, it takes continual prayer, fasting and a feasting on the word of God to rebuild your altar. It takes a lifestyle of sacrifice to follow Him.

PRAY THIS PRAYER WITH ME:
Lord, today I come before you acknowledging, that over time the flames of my altar started to dwindle. At times it seems as if there are no flames left to burn. Father life became tough and situations caused discouragement. But today, I place new hope in you. Today, I choose to dust off the ashes on my altar and replace it with fresh fire. Today, I repent for anything that caused my altar to go out (if you know what those things are, call them out). I renounce every evil covenant working against me. With the blood of Jesus, I dismantle any satanic altar risen up against me or my bloodline. From this day forward, I will offer up a sacrifice of praise on my new altar. I rededicate now my life, my family, and my destiny back to you. I pray this in Jesus name, amen.

CHAPTER 18:

ACCESSING THE POWER OF YOUR ALTAR

Now that you have rebuilt the altar, make good use of its access. The power of your altar depends on the consistency and power of your prayer life. It's been said before, "Little prayer, little power. No prayer, no power. Much prayer, much power"

Prayer is the vehicle that moves heaven. It is the exchange between earth and heaven. We get caught up with events and entertainment and we tend to shy away from prayer sessions. We should be running after prayer, not just publicly but more so in our own personal private time.

The Bible says to pray without ceasing. Prayer is heaven's currency that gives you access to a clear channel that is always available to receive downloads from heaven and ready to upload data from earth to heaven. Prayer brings into alignment, "Thy Kingdom come; Thy will be done in earth as it is in heaven." Prayer gives you access to the heavenly's to pull down to earth what you need here in earth.

One of the things I had to do during this time of warfare was go back to the altar with a different posture. Before, I assumed I knew how to pray, but this time I had to, like the disciples, strip myself of everything I knew and asked the Lord: "Lord, teach me

104

how to pray." I didn't want to pray how I prayed before. I was sick of praying and not seeing results. I didn't want to pray long drawn-out, loud prayers and leave the altar still broken, still empty. I wanted to learn to pray in such a manner that if all I said was two words and never raised my voice, hell felt the impact! I wanted to see the manifestations of what I believed God for.

Everything I've ever done in ministry was conceived, birthed and incubated in prayer. Every download happened there. Then prayer flushed it out until there was manifestation. Each step of the way as the developments happened prayer was consistently bathing the assignment. That is the power of the altar!

However, in this season I was in, I needed to re-learn how to pray. This time my prayer wasn't just about birthing new things. This time around, I had entered a new realm where I needed to learn to fight like I had never fought before. I needed to learn how to pray until hell backed up off my family, finances, ministry! This season was different. The tools and methods I used the previous season were not transferrable. I had to do something different.

The enemy is so accustomed to our routines. We've learned to pray and lead worship a certain type of way. Because it was effective back when, we still use the same methods to fight a completely different war in a different time period. It's like showing up with a VCR in a digital media era. We must make the switch from "what was" to "what is." From "what worked then," to "what works now." Yes, He is the same God yesterday, today and forever. He doesn't change. But the times we are living in has changed. Think about how much our world has changed since 2020. If folks aren't willing to make the switch to the new in business, they are sure to go under. How much more in the kingdom!

So how are we going to know how and when to pivot? Only way is to know is via the altar. I know that method is not for everyone, because some folks have their own agenda for self-promotion. But if we truly want to please the Father, the altar is the only place where we make transactions that connect us with Heaven's agenda. We must connect on the altar to seek His purpose, plan and will. Only there will we receive fresh revelation by consistently communicating with Him to hear what's on His heart.

The power of the altar is that once you get a revelation of it, it provides the blueprint that causes everything in your life to shift and line up according to heaven's design concerning you. It's as we mentioned previously a place of: "Thy kingdom come. Thy will be done on earth as it is in heaven."

Let me say this, even though you have the secrets of the altar, even though the Lord declared it, you must pray it through until it manifests. Pray, decree and declare it until the season shifts. In Daniel chapter 10, we saw where Daniel prayed and fasted for 21 days until the change came. Opposition and delays came but he persisted. He did not get weary in well-doing. Don't allow warfare to cause you to throw in the towel. That's the time more than ever to draw closer to the Lord. Allow your altar to speak louder than your situation.

The secret to prayer is consistency. The Bible says to pray without ceasing (1 Thessalonians 5:16). The more you pray the more you gain access into the heavenly realm. Prayer helps you gain rapport with God where heaven knows your name.

In Luke 18, there was a woman who persistently petitioned an unjust judge, asking him to avenge her of her enemies. This judge had no fear of God or man but because she kept showing up, he granted her petition because he was concerned that she would wear him out. If an unjust judge will do the right thing because of persistency, how much more when we are fervent in prayer to a righteous God. We know James 5:16 says: "The effectual fervent prayer of the righteous availeth much." The word fervent means heartfelt or earnest. Keep praying until you see the manifestation of what God spoke concerning what you prayed for.

Finally, when you pray, remember you have authority to use the name that is above every name, the name of Jesus. Because you are in covenant with Him you can use His name and apply His blood over your marriage, your home, your ministry, your business and so on. When you call on the name of Jesus and apply the blood,demons must back up. They are no match for the God that we serve.

CHAPTER 19:
LISTENING FOR DIVINE INSTRUCTIONS WHILE YOU WAIT

So today as I am writing this section, we are a year separated. That may seem like a short while but for me it feels like an eternity. My heart aches. Sometimes I question whether I should still hold on. What if I "hang in there" and nothing changes? I have been praying this long, will anything change? Only time will tell. Even if the situation doesn't change, I changed because of it. Today I am a better intercessor than I was a year ago. I have discovered my identity and learned the secrets of the kingdom on how to combat the works of the enemy on my new level. Prayer changes everything! And I choose to believe that the Blood still works.

A few weeks before now, I was in my room, and I heard the Lord instruct me to begin to break down the evil altars working against me. I was not sure which specific altars but with instructions, I began to pray in the Holy Ghost! As I prayed, I was instructed to renounce anything in our bloodline that would have afforded an entry way for sin or demonic activity. Immediately, I began to repent of any covenant or agreements made by me or in my bloodline that may have given legal rights to demons to erect an altar or covenant to be erected against me in the demonic world. I prayed against altars that were established in my spouse's bloodline as well.

One of the things I learned during this time, is that legally in the natural as well as in the spiritual, as a spouse you can stand in the gap in prayer *as* your spouse. I did not say for your spouse, I mean as the person. I know this sounds off. But hear me out. One morning the Lord spoke to me and said, "You know you can stand in the gap as your spouse. Because the two of you are joined together as one flesh, when I see him, I see you. When I see you, I see him. You then have legal rights in the natural and in the spirit realm to stand in the gap and petition me as him". He said, for everyone else you can stand in the gap for them but for your spouse you can stand in as them.

Isn't it interesting that even the children a woman carries in her womb is not recognized as one flesh, but a spouse who's joined together in matrimony becomes one? That is why marriage is so sacred and such a phenomenon. Its why God says: "Whom I've joined together let no man put asunder." The only joining with a partner accepted by the Lord is one that is joined in Holy Matrimony. One that's established in covenant with God.

So, per instructions, I spent time warring in the spirit. I prayed until I felt a shift! Then I heard the Lord say now build me an altar. On this altar, I will now establish a new covenant with you.

Now it's important to remember, each time Abraham, Isaac or Jacob had an encounter with God, they would build Him a new altar. The altar represented the meeting place where the encounter happened, whereas it was a place of sacrifice as the covenant was made. It was also a place of worship dedicated to God. The enemy counterfeits what God does. Every time someone comes into agreement with him, a demonic altar is raised. That's why it's important to break down those altars that have been erected against us, that's been plaguing or generations for decades.

So, when the Lord instructed me to raise up a new altar, I was sitting in my bedroom. I thought to myself: "I usually pray in my room, so this is technically my altar area." But as if to answer me in my spirit I heard: "It's not about the altar that was, it's about establishing the new agreement concerning what you just prayed." So immediately I caught on, grabbed my blessed oil and began to anoint my entire home: every bedroom, living room bathroom, kitchen, hallway, etc.! I said: "Lord my entire home is now an altar!" I decided right then and there, that I wanted my entire home to be a place where I could meet Him. No matter where I prayed in my home, not just limited to my bedroom, I would be found on the altar worshiping. If it was my kitchen, I am on the altar. If it is my bathroom, I am still on the altar. No matter where in my home I prayed, I wanted it to be a place for the Lord to show up.

So that night, I dedicated my home and began to worship. The next day, I was feeling good on the inside. It was just a typical day, nothing unusual happening. I left my room and felt like sitting in my couch. I usually don't sit in the living room much. I am not a big tv watcher and so I rarely find a reason to sit there. (I know, I am a bit strange).

So, I wasn't sure why I was just sitting there and didn't quite think too much about it. But now in hindsight is as if I was waiting for something to happen without really knowing. As if I was positioned in a waiting room.

Moments later, I heard a thunderous voice spoke loudly in my right ear saying: "IT JUST BROKE!" As I heard the voice and those words I leaped on my feet and began to shout! It's as if I was waiting for the answer and the answer came. I knew right then and there I had the confirmation that my season had not just shifted, but totally changed!

I couldn't explain it, but I knew my season of testing had ended. I began to run through the house shouting "It broke! It broke!" I was praising God at the top of my lungs. I ran into one of my son's rooms screaming: "It just broke!" He looked at me strange and said "Ok, praise God!" He didn't quite understand what was happening, but he knew his momma and came into agreement with me.

The best way to describe what had happened was that when I sat in the living room, it's as if I was finishing up a final. When I heard the words: "It just broke!" It was equivalent to my professor saying: "You passed the class!" Not just any class, but that one class that I was struggling to get through the entire semester. The class that I thought I was about to fail. I may not have done well on the pop quizzes, exams or special projects. I may have missed some classes or didn't quite understand some of the classroom or homework assignments but because I kept showing up and because I sat through that final, I passed! Now, that class was behind me, and I would not have to EVER repeat it again!

The previous season may have caused some heartaches, some sleepless nights but I made it. I may have wrestled with some witches and warlocks, but I overcame them! I may have cried my eyes out and wanted to throw in the towel, but I made it! I made it because everything the enemy sent my way didn't work! It couldn't take me out! It broke! I was out of that season of testing and made it through in my right mind, and yet still standing by the grace of God. Job said it best and now I understand better: "Though He slay me, yet will I trust in Him…" (Job 13:15A KJV), "…All the days of my appointed time will I wait, Till my change come". (Job 14:14 KJV). My appointed time, my change was here, it came right then, in that very moment.

That following Sunday, the Lord had me to preach a sermon called: "My Season has Shifted!" In the sermon He would have me to share that it didn't matter what it looked like in the now, we must believe by faith that His word is true and if He's declared a shift then believe that there is a shift no matter what the enemy presents in the moment. I don't care what it looks like, I know what God said!

What I mean by this is, there is a set time that we know the seasons change. So, for example, when we know spring has officially started, we may walk outside during that first few weeks and it still feels like winter. It may be very cold. You may still experience snow. The trees may still have no leaves. There may be no birds singing in the trees and the sun may look beautiful, yet you cannot seem to feel the warm rays on your skin. At least not yet. Tell yourself, not yet. In that moment you must remind yourself that it's not what it looks like or what it feels like, it's what you know. It's what God said. Because you trust His voice above what you see, you already know the season shifted so you just have to wait until everything begins to line up.

If you hang in there, just a little while longer, in a few weeks to come or in the months ahead, all the residue from winter, (snow, cold weather, etc.) will have to make its exit. And before long spring will begin to manifest, trees will begin to bloom, the sun will feel warm again and birds will start to sing again in the trees. Soon you will be able to shed the old bulky winter coat. As I'm writing this my spirit is leaping! If you can receive what I'm writing in your spirit, even now a breakthrough is happening in YOU!

I don't know what you've been walking through but even now I decree and declare that "IT" just BROKE in your life. It's no longer winter. Your season just shifted! It's your set time. It's time to dry your eyes and live again. It's time to dream again. It's time to love again. It's time to laugh and dance again. It's your scheduled time to be blessed.

"Thou shalt arise and have mercy upon Zion: for the time to favor her, yea, the set time, is come." (Psalm 102:13).

It's your time to see with your eyes what He has spoken with His lips. It's manifestation time. It's your Kairos moment when heaven stands still to allow everything on earth concerning your situation to line up to God's will concerning you. It's your time of "Thy kingdom come, Thy, will be done in earth as it is in heaven". You ought to shout right there.

CHAPTER 20:
WHILE YOU WAIT…YOU MUST SEE IT BEFORE YOU SEE IT

While waiting on the manifestation of the promise, I was still dealing with some uncomfortable residue from the situation I was in. Feeling frustrated, I asked the Lord a question: "Lord, why is the enemy fighting still me if he's already won?" That's an unusual confession, considering I was "believing" God for the promise. Let's just say in the midst of the stance the enemy came in and I had a moment. Abraham had a moment when he allowed Sarah to talk him into hooking up with Hagar to produce the promise that God promised to him and his wife.

So, in the middle of a frustrating moment, I asked the Lord that question. He didn't answer right away. He waited until my little tantrum had passed, then the next day I heard him answer my question with a question: "Who fights a battle they've already won?" That question left me thinking: "Indeed, who does that?" If the battle is already won, there is no need to keep fighting. Think about it, if you already have victory, you don't keep fighting.

The fact that the enemy is still fighting me, even after I've withdrawn myself from the situation is a clear indication that he KNOWS that he hasn't won. The mere fact that the battle intensified at a time when it should have died out in defeat, is a confirmation that he knows GOD is up to something BIG. He's panicking in fear because he recognizes that he's already defeated. So, at this point, he is making his final attempt to try to frustrate me, to convince me to act out of impulse and to retaliate by doing the opposite of what God already spoke. If I respond accordingly, then I can set things back, even rest the clock on the timing of God. But if I trust God, things will begin to fall into place, and the only defeated foe will be that old serpent, the enemy!

While you wait on the promise, you must remind yourself of what God said to you concerning your situation. Meditate up on that word day and night. Hold dear to the scriptures He's given you to stand on. You must get a vision in your mind of what God promised you and *see it* before you see it. "As a man thinketh in his heart so is he." What you see is what will manifest. The enemy understands this principle quite well and he uses it against us.

One of the things the enemy does is, whenever God speaks a word over our lives, he conjures up a picture of what he wants you to see, which is usually the opposite of what God says. For example, if you received a word that you're about to walk into great wealth, suddenly your bills start hitting your account. He understands the power of sight. He understands that your sight affects your thoughts. He also understands the word which says: "as a man thinketh in his heart so is he." He knows that your thoughts govern your life! He will give you a picture to direct your thoughts to come into agreement with what he wants for you.

Ever consider how when we are hoping for something it's hard to see the end result we want. The picture of the worse seems to pop up instead. That's the enemy trying to conjure up a visual that can cause you to talk oneself out of what God has already decreed and declared What the enemy shows us is always opposite of what God spoke.

So, then the question is: how do you know the picture or thought is from the enemy? You will know if it's attached to fear and/or anxiety. The opposite is also true. How do you know when you have stepped into faith? The picture and/or thought will cause you to experience peace of mind, and there is just something in your knower saying it is going to happen no matter what.

When you understand the principle that nothing is impossible with God, you pray with a different mindset. If nothing is impossible for Him, then you pray knowing that you already have the answer. You can decree and declare because you know it's already done. This then, empowers you to pray from a place of total VICTORY! Glory to God!

From this day forward, start having a visual of what God showed you. Stop meditating on the thoughts or pictures the enemy gives you. They are nothing but mirages to send you in the opposite direction of faith. Instead meditate on what God says.

To meditate means to sit and ponder on. It means to see it in your minds eyes. Go ahead, right now in your mind, begin to think of something you are believing God for. Now, can you see it? Ask yourself: "Whose report do I believe?" Do you believe a master deceiver, or do you believe The Omnipotent God who is integral? The God who has showed up for you repeatedly. The God of the impossible. If you can meditate on God's word long enough, you will begin to see it before you see it. If you can see it in your mind, you will see the manifestation of it. Now watch as it begins to unfold. If I were you I would praise Him now, in advance for the victory.

"Now faith is the substance of thing hoped for, it's the evidence of things not seen." Hebrews 11:1. When walking by faith, there is no plan B or alternative to the outcome. There is only one way out, the desired outcome.

Remember our father, Abraham? God gave him a promise that didn't make sense. Spiritual things do not always make sense. They are not supposed to. He received a promise that he would have a son. God gave him a visual. He told him to look up at the stars in the sky. They were so many he could not even number them. The Lord told him, so it will be with your descendants they will be immeasurable as the stars in the sky. Another time, God told him that his descendants would be as the number of sands by the sea. Now that's some number.

I find this to be interesting because at the time he received the promise, he was old. His body was no longer in a capacity to function to have children. His wife was also old and well beyond the years of childbearing. Yet God made him a promise. Why didn't God show up sooner when they were in their childbearing years?

God's ways are not our ways. He chooses to use ways and methods that sometimes we do not understand to manifest his glory. Sometimes, He waits until the situation is impossible, or it's stinking, really bad, before He steps in. This is so we can learn another side of Him and witness His great power at work. When He shows up like this, there is no shadow of doubt.

When God gave Abraham the visual it helped him to have something to hold on to until the promise manifested. The Bible says in Romans 4:3 "Abraham believed God, and it was counted unto him for righteousness." Because He trusted God's word, his promise to him, he was found in right standing with God. His faith became the catalyst that activated God's promise in his life allowing him to see the tangible manifestation of it.

CHAPTER 21:
HOW THE ENEMY PUSHED BACK AFTER THE DECLARATION CAME

So not long after that declaration came in the previous chapter that: "It Broke!" The enemy sent a breakout assault after that word. Instead of seeing the manifestation, the attack grew stronger. This should not come as a surprise because the enemy's job will always be to try to oppose what God is doing in your life. He knows he can't stop it, but he will attempt to derail it, slow it down, convince YOU to believe the opposite etc.

A secret to the power of the altar is knowing that it's a battleground where the enemy stands defeated. It's a place of answered prayers and victory for the believer. The enemy knows that it's a place where he has no jurisdiction, no access. If he can't access that realm then he can't influence the outcome. Why do you think the enemy fights prayer so much? He wants to keep you on his playing field where he can tear you apart. He knows that on the altar you have angelic assistance. He is no match for the hosts of heaven.

Although I had received the word, there were so many attacks that looked the opposite. It was a tug of war on my faith. I believed the word, but the attacks were painful. I had to cry through some, fight through some, but it was only when I learned to fight God's way that peace came during the storm. It took me a while to utterly understand that the battle wasn't mine, but it was the Lord's, (see 2 Chronicles 20:15). I had to view things from a unique perspective... heaven's perspective.

CHAPTER 22:
HOW I FOUGHT BACK

I fought back by NOT fighting in the natural! I realize that overtime I had developed a fighter spirit… always feeling as though I had to protect or defend myself. For some reason, I would feel unprotected, and because the enemy knew that that was a weak spot, he would send folks who would pick me up and drop me. This showed up in all relationships: friendships, mentorship, family and even in my marriage. There was a constant feeling of being loved, then just when it was getting good, something would happen, and it would end up leaving me feeling rejected.

The lies, persecution and accusations came, but I recognized them to be tests. I had now learned to fight in an unusual way. If you are used to fighting with stick, but then you learn karate; you no longer want to fight with sticks, you will want to use your body to fight back instead.

One day, I woke up thinking: I have always had to protect and defend myself. I am always wrongly accused, misjudged, misunderstood, and mishandled. I felt the spirit of Celie coming on me "All my life I've had to fight." One day, I woke up and I felt the Lord was saying to me, "Forgive all who've hurt you and stop fighting. Stop feeling the need to always defend yourself and your honor. Let folks be folks and think, say, or do whatever they want.

Dust off your feet from the ones who've rejected you. I have accepted you. Stop explaining yourself to those who don't even know why they are being abusive to you. It is not the person, it's those demonic spirits in them working against you. It's time to release it so you can be free." I realized in releasing it, I was taking my power back.

It's funny how if you don't disarm and dismantle the access button the enemy uses against you, he will cause folks to push it every chance they get. It will then ruin your day, your destiny, your life! Jesus told Peter in Luke 22:31-32, "…Simon, Simon, behold, Satan hath desired to have you, that he may sift you as wheat: But I have prayed for thee, that thy faith fail not: and when thou art converted, strengthen thy brethren."

The enemy desires to use situations, circumstances, and people to sift us, to weigh us down and wear us out. He sends frustration to rob us of our peace. If we are not at peace we cannot produce effectively. We could be doing ministry, business, marriage, family but we are not as effective as we could be because we are burdened and frustrated. Because we lack peace, we are barely FUNCTIONING in our role. God can still use us, but we are not as effective.

What the enemy doesn't seem to understand is that the very thing that was meant to take us out is the tool God uses to prune us and make us a better version of ourselves to bring Him glory. Amos 9:9 gives us says it this way: "For I will give the command and will shake Israel along with the other nations as grain is shaken in a sieve, yet not one true kernel will be lost" (NLT). Did you read that last part: "…not one kernel will be lost"! Listen, God will allow it, but it cannot destroy us. The key is to learn the lesson and allow the shaking off of all the debris that the enemy himself placed on us.

The good news is that just like Jesus prayed for Peter, He has also prayed for us. Jesus used the power of the altar to intercede on our behalf. If Jesus stood in the gap for us, who are we to think we do not need to make time to connect with the altar?

And we know that since Jesus prayed for us, His precious blood sprinkled on the altar speaks loudly on our behalf. When the blood speaks, heaven responds. It's a fixed fight! If I were in church, I'd say: "Tell your neighbor it's rigged". Well, take 30 secs anyway and praise Him for the finished work!

So now, here comes the litmus test to see if I was ready to receive the promise. I was recently away doing an assignment when a test came, and can I be honest? I failed miserably. It was at the end of the assignment, and I had some downtime to relax. I was actively minding my business when I received a phone call. The phone call sent me in a spiral as it came from an accusatory standpoint. Something happened and I was accused of being behind the situation. In fact, I had no idea what was happening, and truth is, the person calling really had no right to call me about the situation because in fact it was about my business and not really any of hers. She was defending the other party who was her friend, but because she was caught up in her emotions, she could not discern the truth.

When faced with conflicts, discernment is always needed. Prayer should be the first resort. If confrontation is necessary, please do so under the unction of the Holy Spirit, after you have prayed. Sometimes, He reveals things for one purpose only… so we can PRAY! Discernment will help you rule out the truth from amongst all the lies.

Now, while enjoying my downtime the enemy knew how much this individual's call would ruin my day and he knew who he had full access to the person as a willing, super emotional, non-praying vessel. Sometimes we are too quick to form opinions and judge folks and situations not knowing the truth and because we think we know folks because we have had and "experience" with them. In those moments, we cross boundaries because we are influenced by our emotions. In those moments, we don't stop to pray as we should, instead we just run with information that's laced with some truth. We must remember that the enemy, our adversary is a deceiver, master manipulator and the father of lies seeking to kill, steal and destroy.

Before I knew it, I was in a space defending myself against an attack/bombardment of lies. I was so upset. That quickly, I allowed that spirit to transfer and now the enemy had access to my emotions and my space. That's why the Bible tells us in Proverbs 4:23, "Above all else, guard your heart, for everything you do flows from it". If your heart is guarded, the enemy cannot penetrate it. If it's left unguarded, flowing from it could be the wrong or unnecessary response when situations arise.

Days later, I pondered over the situation and realized all I had to do was hang up and block the person. The person had no legal jurisdiction to even bring those accusations and was only going off what was told to them, which was as I said earlier, lies laced with some truth so it would sound believable. That is what the enemy does. He is a deceiver so he will lace the lies with some truth to cause the undiscerning person to believe. If we do not have the gift of discernment, we can easily be fooled. Discernment cuts through the story and allows you to hear what is not being said and to see what is not being revealed. Discernment says there are some loopholes in this story, some missing parts, or some exaggerated parts.

Discernment also helps you to identify which spirit is speaking: the spirit of God, man, or the enemy.

After I blew up, (ugh), and calmed down I decided to take it to God in prayer. I'm being as transparent as possible because I want to be free, and I want you to be free. I don't want to pretend I get it right every time or pretend that as a leader I don't have "moments". I do. We will, so long as we live in this earthen vessel, but it's what we do in or immediately after that matters. Ask David. He had moments but he dealt with them immediately by repenting.

So, I had to repent for handling it my way. After messing it up miserably, I then chose to hand it over to God.

That is where the POWER OF THE ALTAR comes in, recognizing that the battle really doesn't belong to us. It belongs to the Lord. He's El Gibor who can handle any fight sent our way. Oh yes, He fights for us. Because I was so used to fighting for myself, El Gibor was my last resort. I had to repent and ask Him to step in where I had messed up. He wants to be the Source or the first line of defense we run to when the enemy begins to press our buttons.

On the altar, is where we fight, in prayer, giving heaven access to war on our behalf. That's where we travail and cry out to God. We cannot change situations on our own, because we wrestle not against flesh and blood, but against principalities, against powers, against the rulers of the darkness of this world, against spiritual wickedness in high places.

It may look like you are fighting a person, but you are fighting spirits. Spirits that are manipulating the individual against you. Your posture cannot be retaliation after the individual, but it must be strategic in prayer. Don't get me wrong, because the person availed themselves to be used of the enemy, they're going to get their "reward" for their service. But as Intercessors our response in times of spiritual attack is to seek out the altar.

Now, can I be honest? Sometimes it may look like you are praying but nothing is happening. It may seem like the attacks are coming from the East, the West, the North and the South. It may seem like folks are ganging up against you. It may seem as if El Gibor forgot about you and the enemy is winning. Don't be fooled by what it looks like.His unseen hands are at work behind the scenes fighting a greater battle on your behalf that you cannot see.

God is in the deliverance business. He just doesn't want to deal with the branches… the situation you're immediately caught up in, but He wants to address the root. What is causing the situation? If He doesn't get to the root, you may get rid of the branches, but the root can always re-grow new branches as long as it's still there.

Your altar has POWER to produce results. The altar is the space where, through prayer we give heaven access to our affairs in earth. It's the space where "Thy Kingdom come, thy will be done", Ephesians 6:   It's the space where "whatever you bind on earth will be bound in heaven, and whatever you loose on earth will be loosed in heaven", Matthew 18:18. And it's the space where " You will also decide and decree a thing, and it will be established for you; And the light [of God's favor] will shine upon your ways", Job 22:28

If we understood the power of the altar our entire lives would shift for the better. The enemy would no longer have a foothold or access to us. The altar gives us access to a heavenly realm that allows angels to go to work on our behalf. The problem is that we don't know what we have and so we are fighting battles that angels are assigned to on our behalf. As a people we are destroyed for lack of knowledge.

There are things we face and are challenged by that if we took the time to pray, we would have had angelic assistance working on our behalf. God has set up a system that is proven. It works. It has power and it's the only way to overcome the wiles of the enemy.

Now I must say, when we build an altar, we must submit and subscribe fully to "Thy will be done in earth as it is in heaven." We submit our will to His will. Which means in prayer the outcome may be different than what you expected. But nevertheless, no matter the end result, we know it's His Purpose that prevails. Because He's Sovereign and because He has our best interest at heart and He's a God of integrity, purpose plan and will, we trust His final decisions concerning us. When we learn to yield, He will make it all work out for our good and His glory.

Whatever you may be facing today, your best bet is to create an altar and begin to fight in a different way. Release the natural weapons and take on the spiritual armor described in Ephesians chapter 6, 11-18 and begin to wage war on the enemy. When you fight God's way, it's a win-win!

CHAPTER 23:
THE RESULTS THE ALTAR PRODUCED - THE MANIFESTATION

I woke up one morning and heard myself thanking God for the end results I wanted to see. I began to pray as if the manifestation was in place. As we said earlier, when we pray, we pray from a place of TOTAL VICTORY, a place of IT'S ALREADY DONE! You can't have "wishy-washy" faith. You must believe Hebrews 11:6 "But without faith it is impossible to please Him, for he who comes to God must believe that He is, and that He is a rewarder of those who diligently seek Him."

A few months back, I took a trip to Jamaica. Before leaving the Lord instructed me to print some of my wedding photos and hang them on the wall. I know I heard Him clearly, but decided against it because I was focused on how things seemed to be going in the natural. So in total disobedience, I didn't do it.

Upon my return from the trip, He reminded me again to do it. I was even more reluctant because so much had happened during that time to make me think there was no reason to have hope for restoration. To appease Him, I added the photo to the cart on the website from where I would order but still didn't actually place the order.

Anyhow, months went by and I still hadn't followed through with what God said. So one morning, I woke up and during prayer time, I heard the Lord say, "You still haven't followed my instructions". I said "Ok Lord, I'll do it today". I had intentions at that point to do it but still felt like financially I had a few things I needed to prioritize in the moment. Because I was creating wall canvases, each would be costly so I felt like it could wait until I took care of some other things.

A few minutes later, a phone call came in, the phone call was a friend who on occasion will call to pray for me. She lives in a 3 hour time zone but would call to pray then just hang up, without any conversations. She would do this from time to time as the Lord leads her.

While praying she prophesied that my "prodigal husband is coming home". This was in line with what the Lord instructed me to do. Why else would he want me to print pictures of our wedding day and hang them on my wall?

After she prayed, about an hour later, my phone rang. A friend of mine called to say she has to release the word of the Lord to me. She said, "The Lord said you haven't followed His instructions. He said He wants to restore your marriage, but He gave you instructions a while ago but you have not followed through. He will not do His part until you obey and do your part. Follow His instructions'"

When she said this I laughed, because I knew she was talking about the photos. She then asked me what is it that I am not doing. So, I told her about the photos. I also told her I would do it but I needed to prioritize some stuff first. She then said, "I am sending you the money. Now you have n excuse. Do what He has instructed you to do".

I was cornered. I couldn't make excuses about it anymore. Deep down I was dragging my feet because the enemy kept bringing up the "what if's". I had every reason to consider those because everything in the natural looked opposite. But do you remember what I wrote previously about the power of sight and how important it is to get a glimpse of what God said and stand on that word? Well, this was my test to do just that.

So I went online and ordered the photos. Immediately after the order was officially placed, I received a third unexpected phone call that also confirmed that victory was in motion. God sent three people who had no idea He spoke to me that morning in prayer about my marriage and about following His instructions.

You see, God wanted me to hang the photo on the wall so I could see it. It was a point of contact and a glimpse of what He was getting ready to do. This is truly a faith walk to even pen this information in this book. But as I said to the Lord, I cannot write about the power of the altar and expect others to believe it, if it didn't work for me. I remember at one time, I even wanted to change my last name on the cover of this book to my maiden name, but the Lord instructed me to leave it as is. I choose to obey and like Shadrach, Meshack and Abednego I share the sentiment that no matter the outcome, He is still God! But, I choose to believe our Sovereign God.

Faith ACTIVATES the promise. It's the vehicle through which results are manifested. Your prayer during this time must be very tunnel visioned. You must see only one way out …the finished product. Block everything else the enemy will try to suggest and begin to pray/speak what God has already spoken concerning your situation.

I don't know what you're believing God for, but for example, if you are praying for a marriage to be resuscitated. Pray as follows:

- Begin to worship (we always enter into His presence with thanksgiving and into His courts with praise)

- Lord, I thank you that my marriage is blessed. I thank you that my marriage is whole. My spouse is healed, set free and delivered. (Say their name) have the mind of Christ and is completely whole. His/her heart is soft and pliable and is in love with me. Our love is like a three-fold cord that cannot be broken.

- Lord, I thank you that you are a covenant keeping God. Lord I thank you that our vows are being reactivated. Thank you for being the glue holding us together. I praise you that our love is stronger now than it's ever been. Nothing can separate us from your love of from each other. I thank you that my marriage is now an example of a kingdom marriage: Though we went through great testing in the fire, the fire couldn't consume us. Lord Thank you that Your will in Heaven concerning my marriage is manifested now in earth.

Begin to rejoice as you can see the finished work. You must visualize the end result before you even see it. Close your eyes and begin to see you and your spouse in love and walking in VICTORY. See what already exists in heaven concerning you both. "They Kingdom come, Thy will be done", is now your portion.

Because I know you believe what you just prayed, I'm going to ask you to pause here and take a praise break. Shout because you already have what you prayed for. Now begin to make declarations from the altar, right where you are.

Job 22:28 says: "Thou shalt also decree a thing, and it shall be established unto thee: and the light shall shine upon thy ways." I began to decree that everything around me was lining up with the word of God concerning. Thy Kingdom come; Thy will be done in earth as it is in heaven. Give us THIS DAY our daily bread.

Lord, I thank you that my marriage reflects God's design in heaven. Give us THIS DAY our daily bread. Give it a time period to lineup according to scripture. Command your blessing to line up immediately! Hebrews 11:1 says: "Now faith is the substance of things hoped for, the evidence of things not seen". Use your NOW faith to call things into place this day.

Time doesn't exist on your altar. Your altar gives you access to heaven. It opens up a portal giving access to your blessings immediately. You can access healing, deliverance, favor, anything you desire. Your access to Heaven in that moment in time is what is known as "Kairos moments". Kairos moments are defined as: "God's appointed time to act."

"Thou shalt arise and have mercy upon Zion: For the time to favor her, yea, the set time, is come." Psalm102:13(KJV*)*.

Kairos moments are the set times or appointed times that God uses to favor Zion. It's a divine moment produced by the altar when you can step outside of time into the spirit realm and reach through that heavenly realm to bring back the answer you desire.

Set times are irrevocable…you ought to shout on that! Once in motion they cannot be reversed! Hell can't stop it; people can't stop it. It's a done deal!

So, begin to decree:

Lord, I decree that TODAY is my set time of Favor.
I decree that according to thy word in Psalm 102:13 that … (speak the manifestation you are believing as if it's already done. For example: my sons Andrew, Shemar and Charles are saved and delivered. My body is healed. My marriage is restored etc.).

Fight for what God has given you or has promised you. Even when it doesn't look like what He spoke concerning you. You have the gavel called prayer in your hand, take it to the altar and dismantle the enemy's plans. Pray until you see what God says. As you pray, thank the Lord for the finished work.

Now the question is are you ready for what you prayed for? Can you see it? Oh yes, the promise is here! It is manifestation time.

FINAL WORDS

Writing this book was not planned. It was birthed out of pain. But the Lord promised in Isaiah 66:9, "I will not cause pain without allowing something great to be born." I believe He is an integral God who keeps His promise. This book is the baby birthed from my contractions.

Sometimes we may never understand the ways and methods of God, but I encourage you to trust Him. I always say, "Don't trust the process, trust the Processor." I didn't choose my process. Jeremiah 1:5 says, "before I formed you in the womb I knew you, before you were born I set you apart; I appointed you as a prophet to the nations." God decided who I would be long before I was born. Now the choice was up to me to align my will with His will concerning my life.

Sometimes it takes us going through tough situations to get in line with God's will concerning us. It can be difficult during those times but I'm here to tell you that at the end of my trial, twelve months later, I have a TESTIMONY! I endured the TEST and the TEA and now behold the reward: A book was birthed, my prayer life shifted and my trust in God shot up another dimension. Though I experienced some pain, guess who is still standing saying: "in your face devil, another black eye."

I anticipate there will be even more answered prayers that will come out of this. The results must align with: "Thy Kingdom come. Thy will be done in earth as it is in heaven." I have given my faith a command to "stand still and see the salvation of the Lord. Because I believe what the word says, "Whatever you desire when you pray, believe that you receive it, and you will have it." ~ Mark 11:24

There is power on your altar. Your prayers have the power to shift atmospheres, reverse verdicts in situations, restore/revive dead things etc. Your altar is a place you must sacrifice to get to. Stray away from busyness and the crowd and spend time in prayer on your altar.

The more time you spend praying on the altar the more results you will see. There will be increased exchange in activities between heaven and earth's affairs. You will become a conduit of God's glory being manifested in the earth realm. A conduit of "Thy Kingdom come; Thy will be done in earth as it is in heaven."

I challenge you to not just read this book and just get excited and feel good, but I challenge you to apply what you have learned from it. The information and principles can be applied to any situation that you are facing, not just marriage.

Don't allow yourself to become a prophetic/information junkie. After you've read this book, you have more than enough arsenal to snatch back from the enemy all he stole from you and from your bloodline. What are you waiting for? Go get it!

Remember, those who are most effective in the kingdom are those who operate from the altar. Allow your altar to produce results that not just shift your life, but shifts the lives of your entire generation.

Today I challenge you: If you want to see change, report to the altar. Show up in faith and watch God work!

If at all you have enjoyed this book, look out for my next one coming come: "It's A Love Affair". But in the meantime, if you haven't yet read my first book: "Capturing HerStory", get a copy for you and a friend. I promise it will bless you.

I decree over your life:
A hunger and thirst for the altar
Success in all you set your hands to do
Favor/blessings to overtake you
Wholeness in body, soul and spirit
Healthy Relationships
And the desires of your heart being met, in Jesus mighty name!

www.ingramcontent.com/pod-product-compliance
Lightning Source LLC
Chambersburg PA
CBHW040146160726
48006CB00014B/1636